William Shakespeare
Romeo and Juliet:
Selected Passages

William Shakespeare
Romeo and Juliet: Selected Passages

Herausgegeben von
Ingrid Becker-Ross und Gunthild Porteous-Schwier

Verlagsredaktion
Neil Porter

Layout und technische Umsetzung
Annika Preyhs für Buchgestaltung+, Berlin

Umschlaggestaltung
hawemannundmosch, Konzeption und Gestaltung, Berlin

Photos/Illustrations
Cover: couple: © AISPIX by Image Source/Shutterstock images, balcony: © shootsphoto, Germany/Shutterstock images; p. 11: © akg-images; p. 12: top: © Hannes Geipel, Berlin, bottom: 'Romeo und Julia', Act I, Scene 1, illustration by Moritz Retzsch (1779–1857)/© bpk; p. 14: © Shakespeare's Globe Picture Library/Andy Bradshaw; p. 16: © Hannes Geipel, Berlin; p. 20: Marten Pepyn (1575–1643): 'Ball', ca. 1605, 50 x 64 cm, Moscow, Puschkin Museum/© Artothek; p. 23: © Mary Evans Picture Library/Picture-alliance; p. 25: 'Romeo and Juliet' (1968), Olivia Hussey, Leonard Whiting/© Paramount/The Kobal Collection/Picture-desk; p. 28: © 'Lovers on a Balcony' (watercolour on paper), Barbier, Georges (1882–1932)/Private Collection/the Stapleton Collection/The Bridgman Art Library; pp. 30–31: 'Cassell's Illustrated Shakespeare' (19th century), Frank Dicksee/© Mary Evans Picture Library/Picture-Alliance; p. 44: © Blue Lantern Studio/Corbis (photo), © Arthur Rackham Estate/The Bridgeman Art Library (painting); p. 49: 'Romeo and Juliet', Act III, Scene 1, illustration by John Gilbert (1817–1897), 1856/© akg-images; p. 58: John Taylor (attributed): 'William Shakespeare', ca. 1610, oil on canvas, 55,2 x 43,8 cm, Given by Francis Egerton, 1st Earl of Ellesmere, 1856/© National Portrait Gallery, London; p. 64: 'Romeo and Juliet', 1876 (pen & ink and black chalk), Brown, Ford Madox (1821–1893)/© Bradford Art Galleries and Museums, West Yorkshire, UK/The Bridgeman Art Library; p. 66: 'Romeo and Juliet', Act IV (detail)/© Mary Evans Picture Library/Picture-alliance; p. 82: 'The Death of Romeo and Juliet', final scene of the play by William Shakespeare (1564–1616) (litho), Berty, Maurice (1884–1946)/Private Collection/Archives Charmet/The Bridgeman Art Library; p. 86: 'Romeo und Julia', Act V, Scene 3, illustration by Moritz Retzsch (1779–1857), 1828/© akg-images.

www.cornelsen.de

1. Auflage, 3. Druck 2014

Alle Drucke dieser Auflage sind inhaltlich unverändert und können im Unterricht nebeneinander verwendet werden.

© 2012 Cornelsen Verlag, Berlin
© 2013 Cornelsen Schulverlage GmbH, Berlin

Druck: H. Heenemann, Berlin

ISBN 978-3-06-033102-4

PEFC zertifiziert
Dieses Produkt stammt aus nachhaltig bewirtschafteten Wäldern und kontrollierten Quellen.

www.pefc.de

PEFC/04-31-1156

Abbreviations and Symbols 4

Introduction 5

The Language of Shakespeare 6

The List of Characters 9

ROMEO AND JULIET

Prologue 10

    Infobox: Prologue 10

    Infobox: Iambic pentameter 10

Act I 12

    Infobox: Theatre in Shakespeare's time 14

    Infobox: Marriage and Love 18

    Infobox: Sonnet 24

    Infobox: Alliteration 29

    Infobox: Assonance 29

Act II 30

Act III 46

    Infobox: Dramatic structure 52

    Infobox: Oxymoron 54

    Infobox: William Shakespeare 58

Act IV 66

Act V 74

General Questions on the Play 88

Abbreviations and symbols

AE	American English
adj	adjective
abbr	abbreviation
BE	British English
cf.	confer, see
derog	derogatory
ed.	editor
e.g.	(Latin) exempli gratia = for example
esp.	especially
etc.	(Latin) et cetera = and so on
ff.	and the following lines/pages
fml	formal
i.e.	(Latin) id est = that is
infml	informal
l., ll.	line, lines
n	noun
p., pp.	page, pages
pl	plural
sb.	somebody
sl	slang
sth.	something
usu.	usually
v	verb
vulg	vulgar

INTRODUCTION

William Shakespeare wrote his plays over 400 years ago, yet they still appeal to audiences around the world to this day. Of all Shakespeare's plays, *Romeo and Juliet* is perhaps the best known. It is often classified as the world's most romantic tragic love story, but its real appeal lies in the fact that it is a story full of conflict, gaining life from the continuing changes on stage from hate to love, from hope to death.

It is true that the language of the play is no longer the same as the English which is spoken today, and particularly for students of English as a foreign language there are obstacles to overcome. However, with a bit of help (cf. pp. 6) you will soon find yourself able to understand and even enjoy the sometimes witty, sometimes poetic dialogues and monologues of the play.

You may have come across some modern versions of *Romeo and Juliet.* There are several film versions, the most notable being Baz Luhrmann's *William Shakespeare's Romeo + Juliet* (1996), and Franco Zeffirelli's *Romeo and Juliet* (1968). Other authors have kept the general storyline of the 'star-crossed lovers', but have adapted it to new settings and have used modern English. The best known of these is probably *West Side Story,* a musical by Leonard Bernstein and Stephen Sondheim (1957) which was made into a successful film (1961). What the existence of these versions shows is that the story of Shakespeare's play is a timeless one, adaptable to any generation and, indeed, to any nation in which people erect barriers between groups and forbid members of different groups to fall in love with each other.

Romeo and Juliet is a play made for performance on a stage. This means that the text, while definitely worth studying in its own right, is actually meant as a kind of blueprint for actors. This is why you should try to imagine the scenes on a stage. From time to time you may want to try out some of your ideas for stage directions in the classroom, either as a freeze-frame, or as a more elaborate mini-performance of a short passage.

This book offers a selection of passages from each of the five acts of the original play. This means that your study of the play will focus on the main storyline and characters of *Romeo and Juliet,* leaving out whole scenes or passages in which Shakespeare provided entertainment for the audience (e.g. quarrelling and fighting among the servants of the two feuding families, or rowdy joking among Romeo's friends).

Scene summaries are provided for every single scene in the play to help you find your way in the development of the plot. It is advisable to read and make use of these summaries, because knowing the gist of what happens beforehand will help you understand the way it is told through Shakespeare's dialogues.

There is a list of characters at the beginning; you might find it helpful to copy the character names onto a small sheet of paper you can use as a bookmark while reading, in such a way that you can determine at a glance which of the two sides, or families, a certain character belongs to.

Enjoy your time with Shakespeare's *Romeo and Juliet!*

THE LANGUAGE OF SHAKESPEARE

Shakespeare's language is not easy to understand, not even for a modern-day speaker of English. Since his time the English language has changed quite considerably, so that many words are no longer in use or have the same meaning. However, Shakespeare remains a great influence today and his words still echo down the centuries, as generations have read and enjoyed his plays. And with a little bit of effort his language can still be appreciated today. The annotations on the left-hand pages will offer you the necessary help when reading the play. But it would be useful to be aware of some general points before you start reading; so here are a few tips on how to deal with Shakespeare's language.

Vocabulary

While Shakespeare used many words that are no longer in use in modern English (e.g. 'hinds', I, i, 3, and 'mistempered', I, i, 24) many of the words he used have changed their meaning:

grudge (Prologue, 3)
'Grudge' meant 'quarrel, feud'. Today it means 'feeling of anger towards someone who did something bad to you in the past'. The meaning has only slightly changed, but Shakespeare uses 'grudge' in a way that a modern writer would not.

mutiny (Prologue, 3)
'Mutiny' meant 'dispute, fight'. Today it means 'an open revolt against authority'. Again, the meaning has only slightly changed, but enough to cause confusion to a reader.

Sentence structure

Shakespeare's structure differs from modern English syntax. The positioning of parts of the sentence depended on the emphasis they were given and on the rhythm of the line. As Shakespeare wrote mostly in iambic pentameters, he altered his prose – and often the intonation or pronunciation of words (indicated here by an accent, e.g. 'ĕ') – to make it more suitable to verse. It is worth collecting the words of a sentence and rearranging them in a logical way to understand what the sentence means. Always look for the main verb and the subject first. Here are examples of sentences with an unusual structure:

Some word there was that   *There was some word*
murdered me (III, ii, 40–41)   *that murdered me*

As Shakespeare liked using clauses, his sentences often seem long and complicated. In the Prologue (p. 11), there are only three sentences in 14 lines. That is why it is important to find first the main verb and the subject. In ll. 1–4, the subject is 'two households' and the verb 'break'. If you put the clauses in brackets, the structure becomes clearer:

Two households [subject] *(both alike in dignity) in fair Verona (where we lay our scene) break* [main verb] *from ancient grudge to new mutiny (where* [= which results in] *civil blood makes civil hands unclean)*

In ll. 9–14, the sentence starts with the object (which covers two lines). If the sentence is rewritten with the subject at the beginning, it would read like this (slightly simplified):

The two hours' traffic of our stage [subject] *is* [main verb] *the fearful passage of their death-marked love and the continuance of their parents' rage (which nothing could remove, except their children's end,). If you attend with patient ears to this (i.e. the play that lasts two hours), our toil will strive to fill in what you do not learn here (i.e. in the prologue).*

Note that many of Shakespeare's relative clauses would be separate sentences in modern English. 'Which', etc. is often used to link what could be another sentence onto a previous sentence.

Auxiliary 'do'

In Shakespeare's time, the auxiliary 'do' in interrogative, imperative and negative forms was not always used:

you know not ... (I, i, 2)	*you do not know ...*
why call you ...? (I, i, 13)	*why do you call ...?*
hold me not (I, i, 16)	*don't hold me*
what say you ...? (I, iii, 16)	*what do you say ...?*

On the other hand, the auxiliary 'do' without any special emphasis can be found in positive statements:

she doth teach the torches (I, v, 4)   *she teaches the torches*

Auxiliary 'be'

'Be' as an auxiliary was used to form compound tenses of certain intransitive verbs in Elizabethan English, especially 'come' and 'go' (as is the case in German):

the strangers all are gone (I, v, 104)   *the strangers have all gone*

Second-person pronouns

In 16th-century English there were two forms of 'you':
- 'thou' (object form: 'thee'; possessive determiner: 'thy', 'thine'). In Shakespeare's time subordinates and children were addressed as 'thou' (in the singular). Moreover the common people (and intimate friends) used this form of address amongst themselves.
  Dost thou love me? (II, ii, 90)
  Turn thee, Benvolio, look upon thy death (I, i, 4)

- 'ye/you' (object form: 'you'; possessive determiner: 'your'). In Shakespeare's time 'ye/you' was used as a term of respect for individuals ('Sie'), or as the second-person plural form ('ihr').

It is interesting to note that when Romeo and Juliet first meet (I, v, 53–70), he uses both 'thou' and 'you', while she uses 'you'. Shakespeare is not consistent in how he uses 'you/ye' and 'thou/thee'.

Possessive determiners

In Elizabethan English, 'mine' and 'thine' as possessive determiners were sometimes used instead of 'my' and 'thy' before vowels and 'h'. 'Thine' and 'mine' were also used in much the same way as 'mine' is today (as possessive determiners):

there lies more peril in thine eye (II, ii, 71)

Verb endings

- The third-person singular verb endings: In Shakespeare's time, the third-person singular verb often ended in '-th', e.g. 'doth' (does), 'hath' (has).
- The second-person singular verb endings: In Shakespeare's time, the second-person verb after 'thou' ended in '-st', e.g. 'canst', 'didst', 'camest', 'hast', 'art' (verb: be); or in the case of 'will' and 'shall': 'wilt' and 'shalt'.

– The past participle of some verbs were shortened:
  And find delight writ[ten] there with beauty's pen (I, iii, 19)
  What I have spoke[n] (II, ii, 89)

Would/will

'Would' often means 'want' or 'wish'.
  I would not for the world they saw thee here (II, ii, 74)   *I wouldn't want them to see you here*

Subjunctive

In Elizabethan English the subjunctive was still used.
  Wert thou as far (II, ii, 82)   *If you were as far*
  O, that she knew she were! (II, ii, 11)   *O, if she only knew she was/were*

Compounds

Shakespeare often used compounds to express an idea for which modern English needs a phrase:
  star-crossed (Prologue, 6)   *crossed by the stars*
  death-marked (Prologue, 9)   *marked by death*
  neighbour-stained (I, i, 19)   *stained by* (the blood of) *neighbours*
  world-wearied (V, iii, 25)   *tired of the world*

But

'But' has a variety of meanings, e.g. 'only' 'just', 'without it being the case that …', 'except'.
  but their children's end (Prologue, 11)   *had it not been for their children's end*
  I do but keep the peace (I, i, 5)   *I just/merely keep the peace*
  Be but sworn my love (II, ii, 35)   *if you just swear that you love me*
  'Tis but thy name that is my enemy (II, ii, 38)   *It is only/just your name that is my enemy*
  But that thou overheard'st … (II, ii, 102–103)   *if it had not been for the fact that you overheard …*

Adverbs

For a German some Elizabethan adverbs of place and relative adverbs are easier to understand than for a modern English person.
  thence [dahin]   *wherein* [worin]
  whence [woher]   *wherewith* [womit]
  hence [hierher]   *wherefore* [wofür; weshalb]

Omission of consonant

In order to reflect everyday speech, Shakespeare would leave out consonants (especially the 'v') in particular words.
  e'er   *ever*   *an'*   *and*
  ne'er   *never*   *o'*   *on/of*
  o'er   *over*

THE CHARACTERS

ESCALES	Prince of Verona
MERCUTIO	his kinsman, Romeo's friend
THE COUNTY PARIS	another kinsman, suitor to Juliet (he does not appear in this edition)
MONTAGUE	head of a noble family in Verona which has been at enmity with the Capulets for a long time
LADY MONTAGUE	his wife
ROMEO	his son
BENVOLIO	his nephew, Romeo's friend
BALTHASAR	servant of the Montagues
CAPULET	head of a noble family in Verona which is hostile to the Montagues
LADY CAPULET	his wife
JULIET	his daughter
TYBALT	Lady Capulet's nephew
NURSE	to Juliet
FRIAR LAURENCE	Franciscan friar

THE CHORUS

CITIZENS OF VERONA, MASQUERS, PAGES, SERVANTS, WATCHMEN

Summary

The Chorus sets the scene and gives an overview of the plot, so the audience knows the end in advance.

INFOBOX	Prologue

The Prologue of a Shakespearean play is meant to give the audience a mini-summary of what to expect on stage regarding the plot as well as the performance of it by the acting company.

'Chorus' is a term from Greek drama, in which a group of speakers (a chorus) comments on the action or the individual characters. In *Romeo and Juliet*, the Prologue is usually spoken by the actor who plays the Prince, because he is supposed to stand above the family feud. Only a few of Shakespeare's plays actually have a prologue or chorus.

Notes and annotations

2 *fair:* beautiful
  lay: set
3 *ancient grudge:* Shakespeare never reveals what the feud is about (*grudge:* quarrel)
  mutiny: violence
4 *civil:* of or belonging to citizens
5 *from forth:* born of
  loins: Lenden
6 *star-crossed:* ill-fated (due to the astrological stars)
7 *misadventured piteous overthrows:* unglückselige herzzerreißende Katastrophen
8 *doth:* do (plural)
  strife: Streit, Konflikt
9 *passage:* course
  death-marked: doomed to death
11 *but:* only; except for
  end: death
  nought: nothing
12 *two hours' traffic:* business of two hours
13 *the which:* (reference to the two hours' traffic of the stage)
  attend: listen
14 *here:* reference to the prologue
  toil: work

INFOBOX	Iambic pentameter

Iambic pentameter is a line of five **feet** (a foot being a unit consisting of a group of stressed and unstressed syllables that are repeated in a line) in which an unstressed syllable is followed by a stressed syllable (di dum), a pattern known as an **iamb**. If the lines do not rhyme, it is called **blank verse**. Shakespeare varies the iambic pentameter a great deal, while maintaining the iamb as the most common foot. Here is the first line divided into iambic feet (if you say 'di dum, di dum, di dum, di dum, di dum' first, it may help you feel the rhythm): Two hóuse / holds, bóth / alíke / in díg / nitý

Prologue

Enter CHORUS.

CHORUS: Two households, both alike in dignity,
    In fair Verona, where we lay our scene,
    From ancient grudge break to new mutiny,
    Where civil blood makes civil hands unclean.
5   From forth the fatal loins of these two foes
    A pair of star-crossed lovers take their life.
    Whose misadventured piteous overthrows
    Doth with their death bury their parents' strife.
    The fearful passage of their death-marked love,
10   And the continuance of their parents' rage,
    Which, but their children's end, nought could remove,
    Is now the two hours' traffic of our stage;
    The which if you with patient ears attend,
    What here shall miss, our toil shall strive to mend.

Exit.

1   Study the Prologue and choose which of the sentences below best sums it up.

   ☐ In Verona there was a civil war between two families until two youngsters from the warring families fell in love and decided to kill themselves.

   ☐ The play is about the children of two feuding families who killed each other as they were forbidden from marrying each other.

   ☐ We are going to perform a play that tells the tragic story of two young lovers from families at war with each other, who could only stop their fighting once it had caused their children's death.

2   With a partner, read the Prologue out loud, paying attention to stressed and unstressed syllables as well as any rhymes you detect. The 'Infobox: Iambic pentameter' (p. 10) may help you.

Verona, 16th century

Summary

Benvolio, a Montague, comes across servants of the Montague and Capulet families fighting. He tries to calm the situation, but Tybalt, a Capulet, arrives and increases the tension. A fight starts. The Prince arrives and stops the fight, threatening anyone who is found fighting in the future with death.

Notes and annotations

1 *part:* separate

2 *put up:* put away

• *Tybalt* ['tɪbəlt]

3 *art thou drawn:* is your sword drawn

   heartless hinds [haɪnd]: servants who have no courage (also pun on female deers [hinds] who have no male leader [hart])

6 *manage:* use

9 *have at thee:* warning that he is about to attack

• *fray:* fight

10 *bill, partisan:* types of long spears

• *gown:* dressing gown

13 *crutch:* Krücke

15 *flourish* ['flʌrɪʃ]: schwingen

   spite: defiance

16 *villain:* Schurke

• *train:* attendants

19 *profaner* [prə'feɪnə]: person who abuses sth.

   neighbour-stained steel: swords stained with the blood of neighbours

21 *quench:* löschen

   pernicious: schädlich, bösartig

   rage: uncontrolled anger

22 *issue from:* pour out of

23 *on pain of torture:* with the penalty/punishment of torture (if the Prince is not obeyed)

24 *mistempered:* angry, misused

25 *movèd:* angry

26 *civil:* within the city

   brawl: noisy and ugly fight

   bred of an airy word: which resulted from a trivial remark

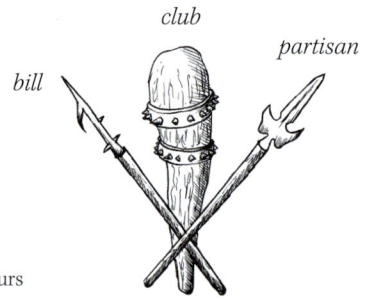
club
partisan
bill

Act I, Scene 1 (extracts)

Verona: a public place

Two servants of the Capulet household began a quarrel with servants of the Montagues and have started fighting.

Servants fighting. Enter BENVOLIO.

BENVOLIO: Part, fools!
　　Put up your swords; you know not what you do.

Beats down the swords of the fighters.

Enter TYBALT.

TYBALT: What, art thou drawn among these heartless hinds?
　　Turn thee, Benvolio, look upon thy death.
5　**BENVOLIO:** I do but keep the peace. Put up thy sword,
　　Or manage it to part these men with me.
　TYBALT: What, drawn, and talk of peace! I hate the word,
　　As I hate hell, all Montagues, and thee.
　　Have at thee, coward!

They fight. Enter several of both houses, who join the fray; then enter citizens, with clubs.

10　**CITIZENS:** Clubs, bills, and partisans! Strike! Beat them down! Down with the
　　Capulets! Down with the Montagues!

Enter CAPULET *in his gown, and* LADY CAPULET.

CAPULET: What noise is this? Give me my long sword, ho!
　LADY CAPULET: A crutch, a crutch! Why call you for a sword?
　CAPULET: My sword, I say! Old Montague is come,
15　And flourishes his blade in spite of me.

Enter MONTAGUE *and* LADY MONTAGUE.

MONTAGUE: Thou villain Capulet! – Hold me not, let me go.
　LADY MONTAGUE: Thou shalt not stir a foot to seek a foe.

Enter PRINCE ESCALES, *with his train.*

PRINCE: Rebellious subjects, enemies to peace,
　　Profaners of this neighbour-stainèd steel, –
20　Will they not hear? – What, ho! You men, you beasts,
　　That quench the fire of your pernicious rage
　　With purple fountains issuing from your veins,
　　On pain of torture, from those bloody hands
　　Throw your mistempered weapons to the ground,
25　And hear the sentence of your movèd prince.
　　Three civil brawls, bred of an airy word,

28 *thrice:* three times

30 throw aside the accessories that make them look respectable
– This could mean things used in their trades or to illustrate their high office.

31 *in hands as old:* in hands that are as old as the partisans

32 which have grown rusty *(cankered)* in peacetime, in order to separate *(part)* the two sides and their malignant *(cankered)* hatred for each other.

34 you will pay with your lives if you break *(forfeit)* this peace

38 *know:* learn of

our further pleasure: what else I intend to do

39 *common judgement-place:* public courtroom

40 *pain of death:* unter Androhung des Todes

INFOBOX   Theatre in Shakespeare's time

When theatre buildings were erected, they had to be outside the city. They were considered immoral places. The Globe Theatre, which was built for the acting company that Shakespeare belonged to (known as the King's Men), was a **round construction** consisting of **three galleries** around an **open-air space**. It was in this open space that most of the audience stood to watch a play. Wealthier spectators could buy seats in the galleries. Play-going was popular, even among poor people, as it was the only entertainment available, which is why theatres got a reputation for being noisy and rowdy places. The **stage**, which had a roof of its own, extended far into the open space, so that the people actually stood around it on three sides. There was usually an upper gallery like a balcony, from which actors could also speak. There was no lighting, so the plays had to be performed in daylight, and there were very few stage props. This is why characters in Shakespeare's plays often describe the time of day as well as the scenery they are meant to be acting in. Another particularity of the Elizabethan theatre was the fact that women were not allowed to act, i.e. all female parts were played by boys and men.

By thee, old Capulet, and Montague,
Have thrice disturbed the quiet of our streets,
And made Verona's ancient citizens
30 Cast by their grave-beseeming ornaments,
To wield old partisans, in hands as old,
Cankered with peace, to part your cankered hate.
If ever you disturb our streets again,
Your lives shall pay the forfeit of the peace.
35 For this time, all the rest depart away.
You, Capulet, shall go along with me,
And, Montague, come you this afternoon,
To know our further pleasure in this case,
To old Free-town, our common judgment-place.
40 Once more, on pain of death, all men depart.

*Montague asks Benvolio about the cause of the fight and then asks where his
son Romeo has been. Benvolio tells the Montagues that Romeo prefers being
alone to being with his friends. Romeo arrives and confides to Benvolio that
he is in love, but that his loved one, a lady called Rosaline, does not return his
feelings.*

1 Listing

The action of the play begins with a street fight among members of the two households.
Identify the steps that lead from the servants' quarrel at the beginning of the scene to the Prince's
threat in ll. 34–35.

Step 1: The servants start fighting in the street.

Step 2: _____

Step 3: _____

Step 4: _____

Step 5: _____

Step 6: _____

2 Discuss the effectiveness of such a beginning for a stage introduction of the 'ancient grudge' between
the households in question. (Link your ideas to what you know about audiences and theatres in
Shakespeare's time; cf. 'Infobox: Theatre in Shakespeare's time', p. 14)

Summary

In this extract Lady Capulet tells her 14-year-old daughter that Count Paris wants to marry her, and asks her to pay attention to him at the feast and decide whether she would like to have him as her husband.

Notes and annotations

2 what do you think about getting married?

4 *were ... only nurse:* if I were not the only nurse you had

Note, ll. 4–5: The nurse is praising Juliet for her wisdom in seeing marriage as being an honour.

7 *ladies of esteem:* ladies from good families

9 *much upon these years:* at about the same age

11 *valiant:* brave and good

13 *a man of wax:* so good looking he looks like a wax sculpture

15 *in faith:* indeed

17 *behold:* see

Note, ll. 18–29: Lady Capulet uses the metaphor of a book (*volume:* Band) to explain how Juliet should examine Paris. Notice the use of rhyming couplets here.

19 *writ:* written

20 *married lineament:* feature/line which is in harmony with others

21 *how one another lends content:* how each (feature) fits in with the other

23 *margent:* margin

24 *unbound:* (of a book) without a cover; (of a man) without a wife

26 *the fish lives in the sea:* just as the fish is at home surrounded by water

26–27 *and 'tis much pride ... to hide:* so it makes (a woman) proud to have a beautiful exterior *(fair without)* which surrounds / is wrapped around *(hide)* a beautiful interior *(fair within)*

28 *many's eyes:* the eyes of many people

29 *clasps:* Verschlüsse, Spangen

31 *making yourself no less:* not making yourself lower in social standing (i.e. it is a good marriage for her status)

Act I, Scene 3 (extracts)

In Act I, Scene 2, the Count of Paris asks Capulet for Juliet's hand in marriage. Capulet invites Paris to a feast at their house that evening; he sends a servant out to invite other guests to the feast. The illiterate servant comes across Benvolio and Romeo, and asks Romeo to read out the list of guests for him. When Romeo discovers that his beloved Rosaline is on that list, he decides to go there as well, incognito.

At the beginning of this scene Lady Capulet has asked the Nurse to fetch Juliet, but the Nurse keeps telling stories about Juliet as a little girl.

A room in Capulet's house.

LADY CAPULET *and the* NURSE. *Enter* JULIET.

LADY CAPULET: Tell me, daughter Juliet,
　　How stands your disposition to be married?
JULIET: It is an honour that I dream not of.
NURSE: An honour! Were not I thine only nurse,
5　　I would say thou hadst sucked wisdom from thy teat.
LADY CAPULET: Well, think of marriage now; younger than you,
　　Here in Verona, ladies of esteem,
　　Are made already mothers: by my count,
　　I was your mother much upon these years
10　　That you are now a maid. Thus then in brief:
　　The valiant Paris seeks you for his love.
NURSE: A man, young lady! Lady, such a man
　　As all the world – why, he's a man of wax.
LADY CAPULET: Verona's summer hath not such a flower.
15 **NURSE:** Nay, he's a flower; in faith, a very flower.
　　LADY CAPULET: What say you? Can you love the gentleman?
　　This night you shall behold him at our feast;
　　Read o'er the volume of young Paris' face,
　　And find delight writ there with beauty's pen;
20　　Examine every married lineament,
　　And see how one another lends content
　　And what obscured in this fair volume lies
　　Find written in the margent of his eyes.
　　This precious book of love, this unbound lover,
25　　To beautify him, only lacks a cover:
　　The fish lives in the sea, and 'tis much pride
　　For fair without the fair within to hide:
　　That book in many's eyes doth share the glory,
　　That in gold clasps locks in the golden story.
30　　So shall you share all that he doth possess,
　　By having him, making yourself no less.

32 *women grow by men:* men make women get bigger (i.e. pregnant)

33 *can you like of:* do you think you could approve of / be pleased with

34 I'll try/expect to like him if looking is enough to make me like him

35 *endart:* pierce like a dart

36 than you allow it to do so

INFOBOX	Marriage and love

In Shakespeare's time women married early, usually in their early 20s, if not earlier. Usually, wealthy families would arrange marriages between their children. While love often played a role in relationships, sexual relations were considered taboo for women. Sex outside marriage would result in a woman losing her honour and becoming unmarriageable.

NURSE: No less! Nay, bigger! Women grow by men.
LADY CAPULET: Speak briefly, can you like of Paris' love?
JULIET: I'll look to like, if looking liking move.
35   But no more deep will I endart mine eye
        Than your consent gives strength to make it fly.

1 Describe the impressions you get of the three characters with regard to their views on marriage, and on Paris as a suitor in particular.

2 Analyse how Lady Capulet uses the metaphor of a book to describe Paris in ll. 18–29. Identify the relevant key words and explain what they stand for.

Summary

Romeo and Juliet meet for the first time, and fall in love. Tybalt wants to start a fight when he recognizes Romeo, but Capulet prevents him. Both Romeo and Juliet separately question Juliet's Nurse about each other and discover who the other is.

Note and annotations

  1 *enrich the hand:* make the hand look better

  2 *of yonder knight:* of that young man over there

  6 *Ethiop:* African

  8 *shows:* appears

     trooping with: being among, associating with

10 *the measure done:* once this dance is over

     her place of stand: the place where she stands

11 *rude:* rough, primitive, ungraceful

12 *forswear:* deny

15 *rapier* ['reɪpɪə]: type of sword

16 *hither:* hierher

     antic face: comic mask

17 *fleer:* laugh in a nasty way, sneer

     scorn at: mit Verachtung betrachten

     solemnity: celebration; feast

18 *by the stock and honour of my kin:* by the honourable breeding of my family

19 *hold:* consider

20 *wherefore:* why

22 *spite:* Trotz

23 *content thee:* calm down

25 *coz:* cousin

26 *he bears him:* he carries himself; he behaves

     portly: dignified

27 *to say truth:* to tell the truth; in fact

     brags of: boasts of; speaks very well of

28 *to be:* as being; that he is

     well-governed: well-behaved

30 *do him disparagement:* treat him with disrespect

33 *show a fair presence:* behave well

     frowns: Stirnrunzeln

34 *ill-beseeming semblance:* inappropriate appearance

Act I, Scene 5 (extracts)

Romeo and his friends arrive in front of Capulet's house for the party. Mercutio tries to cheer Romeo up, who has had a bad dream and thinks it is not wise to go to the feast. Mercutio makes fun of Romeo's belief in his dream, but Romeo is sure that some terrible fate awaits him. Nevertheless, he goes to the party with his friends, where he sees Juliet.

A hall in Capulet's house.

Enter CAPULET *and* TYBALT, ROMEO *and* BENVOLIO, *and other guests.*

ROMEO: *[To a* SERVANT*]* What lady is that, which doth enrich the hand
    Of yonder knight?
SERVANT: I know not, sir.
ROMEO: O, she doth teach the torches to burn bright!
5   It seems she hangs upon the cheek of night
    Like a rich jewel in an Ethiop's ear.
    Beauty too rich for use, for earth too dear.
    So shows a snowy dove trooping with crows,
    As yonder lady o'er her fellows shows.
10   The measure done, I'll watch her place of stand,
    And, touching hers, make blessèd my rude hand.
    Did my heart love till now? Forswear it, sight!
    For I ne'er saw true beauty till this night.
TYBALT: This, by his voice, should be a Montague.
15   Fetch me my rapier, boy. What dares the slave
    Come hither, covered with an antic face,
    To fleer and scorn at our solemnity?
    Now, by the stock and honour of my kin,
    To strike him dead, I hold it not a sin.
20 CAPULET: Why, how now, kinsman! Wherefore storm you so?
TYBALT: Uncle, this is a Montague, our foe,
    A villain that is hither come in spite,
    To scorn at our solemnity this night.
CAPULET: Young Romeo is it?
TYBALT: 'Tis he, that villain Romeo.
25 CAPULET: Content thee, gentle coz, let him alone.
    He bears him like a portly gentleman.
    And, to say truth, Verona brags of him
    To be a virtuous and well-governed youth.
    I would not for the wealth of all the town
30   Here in my house do him disparagement.
    Therefore be patient, take no note of him:
    It is my will, the which if thou respect,
    Show a fair presence and put off these frowns
    And ill-beseeming semblance for a feast.

36 *endure:* put up with

Note, l. 37: a goodman is a rank below that of a gentleman. With *goodman* and *boy* Capulet is insulting Tybalt in a way that only the head of the household could.

37 *go to:* expression of shock or surprise

39 *God shall mend my soul!:* May God save my soul!

40 *mutiny:* Meuterei

41 *set cock-a-hoop:* cause disorder by your high spirits

    You'll be the man!: You want to be the person giving orders!

42 *shame:* dishonour

43 *saucy:* badly behaved

44 This behaviour of yours may have negative consequences for you, indeed

45 *contrary:* contradict, oppose

    marry: expression of surprise or annoyance

Note, ll. 45–48: Capulet is addressing his guests and, privately, Tybalt.

46 *princox:* arrogant young man

48 *cheerly:* with joy

50–51 Being forced to be patient while being obstinately angry *(choler)* makes my body shake as these opposing forces meet each other.

51 *withdraw:* retire; leave

52 *gall:* poison

35 **TYBALT:** It fits, when such a villain is a guest:
     I'll not endure him.
  CAPULET: He shall be endured:
     What, goodman boy! I say, he shall! Go to!
     Am I the master here, or you? Go to!
     You'll not endure him! God shall mend my soul!
40   You'll make a mutiny among my guests!
     You will set cock-a-hoop! You'll be the man!
  TYBALT: Why, uncle, 'tis a shame.
  CAPULET: Go to, go to!
     You are a saucy boy; is't so, indeed?
     This trick may chance to scathe you, I know what.
45   You must contrary me! Marry, 'tis time. –
     Well said, my hearts! – You are a princox; go!
     Be quiet, or – More light, more light! – For shame!
     I'll make you quiet, what! – Cheerly, my hearts!
  TYBALT: Patience perforce with wilful choler meeting
50   Makes my flesh tremble in their different greeting.
     I will withdraw, but this intrusion shall
     Now seeming sweet convert to bitter gall.

Exit.

Note, ll. 53–66: These 14 lines are a sonnet. Besides the formal features of the sonnet
form, these lines, which are the first spoken between Romeo and Juliet, are
separated from the others, firstly by Tybalt's double couplets (ll. 49–52), which
mark a conclusion (emphasized by his leaving the stage) and the kiss which takes
place after l. 66.
Romeo uses the language of religious pilgrimage to describe his approach to Juliet's
lips.

| **INFOBOX** | **Sonnet** |

A sonnet is a 14-line poem in iambic pentameter. Shakespeare's sonnets use the **rhyme scheme**
abab cdcd efef gg. The three **quatrains** can be linked together through content or in argument in a
variety of ways, but often there is a **'volta'** (or turn) in the course of the argument after the second
quatrain. The final **couplet** often provides an opportunity to sum up the argument of the poem
with an epigram. Normally a sonnet is written about a loved one. Shakespeare makes use of the
sonnet form in *Romeo and Juliet* in an unusual way: he turns it into a dialogue between two lovers.
Besides the sonnet here, the Prologue (p. 11) is also a sonnet.

---

53 *profane:* dishonour, make unholy

54 *shrine:* Heiligtum, Pilgerstätte (Romeo is referring to her hand.)

the gentle sin is this: this is merely a mild sin

55 *blushing:* turning red with embarrassment; modest

57 *wrong:* speak badly and truthfully about

58 which shows proper devotion *(= Andacht; Hingabe)* by doing this *(i.e. touching my hand)*

Note, l. 60: A palmer was a pilgrim who had returned from the Holy Land, in sign of
which he carried a palm-branch or -leaf. Juliet puns on the words 'palmer' and
'palm', suggesting that the pilgrim shows devotion by using his hand (or palm) to
touch holy relics.

64 *grant thou:* give me what I pray for

Note, l. 65: Juliet puts herself into the role of the statue of a saint, which does not
move but will grant the wishes of the devotee; in other words, she is telling him he
must make the first move and kiss her.

67 *purged:* cleansed, purified, removed

69 *o trespass sweetly urged:* such a beautiful encouragement to commit a sin *(trespass)*

70 *by the book:* very well, as if you had studied kissing

71 *craves:* desires

ROMEO: *[To* JULIET*]* If I profane with my unworthiest hand
　　　This holy shrine, the gentle sin is this.
55　　My lips, two blushing pilgrims, ready stand
　　　To smooth that rough touch with a tender kiss.
JULIET: Good pilgrim, you do wrong your hand too much,
　　　Which mannerly devotion shows in this;
　　　For saints have hands that pilgrims' hands do touch,
60　　And palm to palm is holy palmers' kiss.
ROMEO: Have not saints lips, and holy palmers too?
JULIET: Ay, pilgrim, lips that they must use in prayer.
ROMEO: O, then, dear saint, let lips do what hands do:
　　　They pray; grant thou, lest faith turn to despair.
65 JULIET: Saints do not move, though grant for prayers' sake.
ROMEO: Then move not, while my prayer's effect I take.

He kisses her.

　　　Thus from my lips, by yours, my sin is purged.
JULIET: Then have my lips the sin that they have took.
ROMEO: Sin from thy lips? O trespass sweetly urged!
70　　Give me my sin again.

He kisses her again.

JULIET:　　　　　　　　You kiss by the book.
NURSE: Madam, your mother craves a word with you.

72 *bachelor:* young unmarried man

74 *virtuous:* tugendhaft

75 *that you talked withal:* who you talked with

76 *lay hold of:* win over; marry

77 *the chinks:* lots of money

Note, l. 78: Romeo takes up the Nurse's statement about money and uses words from the field of money to express his unhappiness that Juliet is a Capulet.
   (dear account: teure Berechnung)

79 come on, let's go, when the fun is at its best

80 *the more is my unrest:* if I stay longer, I will feel more uncomfortable

82 *trifling foolish:* small modest

   towards: soon

Note, l. 83: Obviously Romeo and his friends have made their excuses so that they can leave.

83 *e'en = even:* really

86 *fay:* faith

   it waxes late: it is getting late

88 *yond …:* that … over there

95 *like:* likely

98 *sprung:* entsprungen

99 I got to see him too early and found out who he is too late!

100 *prodigious:* ominous

102 *even:* just

103 *of:* from

   •   *within:* offstage

ROMEO: What is her mother?

NURSE: Marry, bachelor,
Her mother is the lady of the house,
And a good lady, and a wise and virtuous
75   I nursed her daughter, that you talked withal;
I tell you, he that can lay hold of her
Shall have the chinks.

ROMEO: Is she a Capulet?
O dear account! My life is my foe's debt.

BENVOLIO: Away, begone, the sport is at the best.

80   **ROMEO:** Ay, so I fear; the more is my unrest.

CAPULET: Nay, gentlemen, prepare not to be gone;
We have a trifling foolish banquet towards.

They whisper in his ear.

Is it e'en so? Why, then, I thank you all.
I thank you, honest gentlemen; good night.
85   More torches here! Come on then, let's to bed.
Ah, sirrah, by my fay, it waxes late.
I'll to my rest.

Exeunt all but JULIET *and* NURSE.

JULIET: Come hither, nurse. What is yond gentleman?

NURSE: The son and heir of old Tiberio.

90   **JULIET:** What's he that now is going out of door?

NURSE: Marry, that, I think, be young Petrucio.

JULIET: What's he that follows there, that would not dance?

NURSE: I know not.

JULIET: Go ask his name – if he be marrièd,
95   My grave is like to be my wedding bed.

NURSE: His name is Romeo, and a Montague;
The only son of your great enemy.

JULIET: My only love sprung from my only hate!
Too early seen unknown, and known too late!
100   Prodigious birth of love it is to me,
That I must love a loathèd enemy.

NURSE: What's this? What's this?

JULIET: A rhyme I learned even now
Of one I danced withal.

One calls within 'Juliet'.

NURSE: Anon, anon!
Come, let's away; the strangers all are gone.

Exeunt.

1 **Multiple Choice**

Which of the following does Romeo mean in l. 4? Tick the correct box.

☐ She knows how to light up a room with torches.

☐ She is clever at lighting torches.

☐ Her beauty is brighter than torchlight.

☐ Whenever she walks into a room, her presence lights it up.

2 Read Romeo's speech in ll. 4–13 out aloud, paying attention to sound devices such as alliteration, assonance and rhyme. What is the effect of these devices especially in a speech on stage?

INFOBOX	Alliteration

Alliteration is the repetition of consonants at the beginning of neighbouring words or of stressed syllables within neighbouring words.
Example: **A**round the **r**ugged **r**ock the **r**agged **r**ascal **r**an.

INFOBOX	Assonance

Assonance is the repetition of the same or similar vowel sounds within stressed syllables of neighbouring words.
Example: the p**o**ppies bl**o**w between the cr**o**sses, r**o**w on r**o**w

3 **a)** Explain and comment on Tybalt's urge to kill Romeo on the one hand, and his uncle Capulet's reasons for preventing this on the other hand (ll. 14–52).

b) Compare Tybalt's reactions in this scene with his behaviour in Act I, Scene 1.

4 Look at Romeo's and Juliet's exchange (ll. 53–70) and study the imagery the speakers use.

a) Determine the fields the images belong to, and discuss how these fields are combined.

b) Describe the role that Romeo ascribes to Juliet by using this imagery, and the way Juliet reacts to his manner of addressing her.

c) Now look at the form in which they speak with each other in ll. 53–66, examining the ways the lines are divided up between them and how the rhymes work.

d) Explain how this text is unusual in the way it is presented (cf. 'Infobox: Sonnet', p. 24, for help).

5 Write a newspaper article based on what you as a reporter saw at the Capulets' party, including the necessary background information.

Summary

Romeo is outside Juliet's house when she appears and talks aloud about her feelings for Romeo, unaware that he is listening. He then reveals himself, and they speak of their mutual feelings. They arrange to get married.

Notes and annotations

 1 A person who makes fun of the scars (of others) has never had his own feelings hurt

 2 *yonder:* that ... over there

 4 *envious:* neidisch

 6 *her maid:* the servant of Diana, the goddess of the moon and virginity

 7 *maid:* here, the reference is to Juliet's virginity

 8 *vestal livery* ['lɪvəri]: virginal uniform

 11 O, if only she knew she were my love

 13 *discourses:* speaks; looks around

 15–17 two of the most beautiful stars must leave for a time and ask her eyes to twinkle (= *funkeln*) in their orbits until they return

 18 *they:* (and) the two stars (were)

 21 *airy region:* sky

     stream: send beams of light

Act II, Scene 2

In the previous scene Romeo reveals that he has fallen in love with Juliet and hides from his friends. They look for him and make fun of his passion, believing it is for Rosaline. He returns to the Capulet house.

Capulet's orchard.

Enter ROMEO.

ROMEO: He jests at scars that never felt a wound.
But, soft! What light through yonder window breaks?
It is the east, and Juliet is the sun.
Arise, fair sun, and kill the envious moon,
5   Who is already sick and pale with grief,
That thou, her maid, art far more fair than she.
Be not her maid, since she is envious;
Her vestal livery is but sick and green
And none but fools do wear it; cast it off.

Enter JULIET *above.*

10   It is my lady, O, it is my love!
O, that she knew she were!
She speaks yet she says nothing: what of that?
Her eye discourses; I will answer it.
I am too bold, 'tis not to me she speaks.
15   Two of the fairest stars in all the heaven,
Having some business, do entreat her eyes
To twinkle in their spheres till they return.
What if her eyes were there, they in her head?
The brightness of her cheek would shame those stars,
20   As daylight doth a lamp; her eyes in heaven
Would through the airy region stream so bright
That birds would sing and think it were not night.

28 *a winged messenger of heaven:* an angel

29–30 to the amazed eyes that show their whites as mortals gaze upwards at him

31 *bestrides:* stands on top of

  lazy-puffing: slow moving

33 *wherefore:* why

34 *deny your father:* refuse to acknowledge who your father is

35 *be but sworn my love:* if you swear that you love me

38 *'tis but:* it is only

39 *though not a Montague:* even if you were not a Montague

46 *owes:* owns, has

47 *title:* name

  doff: get rid of, remove, throw away

48 *for:* in exchange, in return for

50 *call me but love:* just call me your love

  baptised: getauft

51 *henceforth:* from now on

52 *bescreened:* hidden

53 *stumblest on my counsel:* intrude on my private thoughts

59 *utterance:* Sprechen

61 *thee dislike:* make you unhappy

See, how she leans her cheek upon her hand!
O, that I were a glove upon that hand,
25   That I might touch that cheek!
JULIET: Ay me!
ROMEO: *[Aside]*   She speaks.
O, speak again, bright angel! For thou art
As glorious to this night, being o'er my head,
As is a wingèd messenger of heaven
Unto the white-upturnèd wond'ring eyes
30   Of mortals that fall back to gaze on him
When he bestrides the lazy-puffing clouds
And sails upon the bosom of the air.
JULIET: O Romeo, Romeo! Wherefore art thou Romeo?
Deny thy father and refuse thy name;
35   Or, if thou wilt not, be but sworn my love,
And I'll no longer be a Capulet.
ROMEO: *[Aside]* Shall I hear more, or shall I speak at this?
JULIET: 'Tis but thy name that is my enemy.
Thou art thyself, though not a Montague.
40   What's Montague? It is nor hand, nor foot,
Nor arm, nor face, nor any other part
Belonging to a man. O, be some other name!
What's in a name? That which we call a rose
By any other name would smell as sweet;
45   So Romeo would, were he not Romeo called,
Retain that dear perfection which he owes
Without that title. Romeo, doff thy name,
And for that name which is no part of thee
Take all myself.
ROMEO: I take thee at thy word:
50   Call me but love, and I'll be new baptised;
Henceforth I never will be Romeo.
JULIET: What man art thou that thus bescreened in night
So stumblest on my counsel?
ROMEO: By a name
I know not how to tell thee who I am:
55   My name, dear saint, is hateful to myself,
Because it is an enemy to thee;
Had I it written, I would tear the word.
JULIET: My ears have not yet drunk a hundred words
Of that tongue's utterance, yet I know the sound:
60   Art thou not Romeo and a Montague?
ROMEO: Neither, fair saint, if either thee dislike.
JULIET: How camest thou hither, tell me, and wherefore?
The orchard walls are high and hard to climb,
And the place death, considering who thou art,
65   If any of my kinsmen find thee here.

66 *o'erperch:* fly over

67 *limits:* boundaries

69 *stop:* Hindernis

71 *peril:* danger

72–73 *look thou … enmity:* if you look at me with sweetness, I am protected against their enmity *(= Feindschaft)*

74 *not for the world:* not for anything at all

75 *cloak:* Mantel

76 *but:* unless

78 *prorogued:* postponed

 wanting of: lacking

81 *counsel:* advice

82 *pilot:* ship's navigator

83 *vast:* enormous, very wide

84 *adventure:* travel (in search of goods)

86 *maiden:* young girl's

 bepaint: colour, make red, paint

88 *fain:* gladly

 dwell on form: observe the rules of proper behaviour

89 *compliment:* phrases used between men and women who do not know each other well

 – Juliet says she would normally have kept up the formal rules of behaviour, but as her thoughts are known, she may as well say goodbye to conventions and be truthful.

90 *ay:* yes

91 *swear'st:* swear (that you love me)

92–93 *at lovers' perjuries they say Jove laughs:* it is said that Jove (= Jupiter) laughs at the lies lovers tell (as it happens all the time)

Note, ll. 96–97: Juliet reminds the audience of how a young woman was supposed to react to the courting of a young man: frowning (i.e. looking displeased or uninterested) and rejecting the young man *(and say thee nay)*. This will allow him to continue to woo (= umwerben) her.

97 *but else, not for the world:* but otherwise, I would rather not do so for anything at all

98 *fond:* infatuated; foolish; tender-hearted

99 *light:* morally loose, improper

100 *true:* constant, faithful

101 *coying to be strange:* pretending in a cunning way to be different from what they are

102 *strange:* distant, reserved

103 *but that:* if it had not been for the fact that

 ere: before

 ware: aware

105 and do not consider (*impute:* unterstellen) that my easy giving in to you (*yielding:* Nachgeben) is due to false feelings

106 *which:* refers to 'yielding'

 discovered: revealed

Note, ll. 107–109: Romeo is about to come out with more typical phrases of love. Juliet cuts him short. Having had her feelings discovered, she is obviously in no mood to have Romeo express his feelings in characteristic phrases.

ROMEO: With love's light wings did I o'erperch these walls;
    For stony limits cannot hold love out,
    And what love can do, that dares love attempt.
    Therefore thy kinsmen are no stop to me.

70 JULIET: If they do see thee, they will murder thee.

ROMEO: Alack, there lies more peril in thine eye
    Than twenty of their swords: look thou but sweet,
    And I am proof against their enmity.

JULIET: I would not for the world they saw thee here.

75 ROMEO: I have night's cloak to hide me from their sight.
    And but thou love me, let them find me here.
    My life were better ended by their hate,
    Than death proroguèd, wanting of thy love.

JULIET: By whose direction found'st thou out this place?

80 ROMEO: By love, who first did prompt me to inquire;
    He lent me counsel and I lent him eyes.
    I am no pilot, yet, wert thou as far
    As that vast shore washed with the farthest sea,
    I would adventure for such merchandise.

85 JULIET: Thou know'st the mask of night is on my face,
    Else would a maiden blush bepaint my cheek
    For that which thou hast heard me speak tonight.
    Fain would I dwell on form, fain, fain deny
    What I have spoke, but farewell compliment!
90   Dost thou love me? I know thou wilt say 'Ay',
    And I will take thy word: yet if thou swear'st,
    Thou mayst prove false. At lovers' perjuries
    They say Jove laughs. O gentle Romeo,
    If thou dost love, pronounce it faithfully:
95   Or if thou think'st I am too quickly won,
    I'll frown and be perverse and say thee nay,
    So thou wilt woo. But else, not for the world.
    In truth, fair Montague, I am too fond,
    And therefore thou mayst think my behaviour light.
100   But trust me, gentleman, I'll prove more true
    Than those that have more coying to be strange.
    I should have been more strange, I must confess,
    But that thou overheard'st, ere I was ware,
    My true love's passion. Therefore pardon me,
105   And not impute this yielding to light love,
    Which the dark night hath so discoverèd.

ROMEO: Lady, by yonder blessèd moon I swear
    That tips with silver all these fruit-tree tops –

109 *inconstant:* changing

110 *circled orb:* sphere in which the moon circles the earth

114 *idolatry:* Vergötterung; Götzenverehrung

116 *joy:* rejoice

117 *contract:* exchange of lover's vows

118 *unadvised:* done without careful consideration

121 *bud:* Knospe

122 *beauteous:* beautiful

129 *would:* wish

131 *frank:* truthful; generous

133 *bounty:* generosity

   boundless: deep, unending

137 *anon:* I am coming

139 *am afeared:* am afraid, fear

141 *flattering-sweet:* delightfully attractive

   substantial: real

142 let me say a few more words, Romeo, and then it will indeed be 'good night'

143 *bent:* intention

145 *one that I'll procure:* somebody who I will engage as a messenger

JULIET: O, swear not by the moon, the inconstant moon,
110   That monthly changes in her circled orb,
        Lest that thy love prove likewise variable.
ROMEO: What shall I swear by?
JULIET: Do not swear at all;
        Or, if thou wilt, swear by thy gracious self,
        Which is the god of my idolatry,
115   And I'll believe thee.
ROMEO: If my heart's dear love –
JULIET: Well, do not swear. Although I joy in thee,
        I have no joy of this contract tonight.
        It is too rash, too unadvised, too sudden;
        Too like the lightning, which doth cease to be
120   Ere one can say 'It lightens'. Sweet, good night!
        This bud of love, by summer's ripening breath,
        May prove a beauteous flower when next we meet.
        Good night, good night! As sweet repose and rest
        Come to thy heart as that within my breast!
125 **ROMEO:** O, wilt thou leave me so unsatisfied?
JULIET: What satisfaction canst thou have tonight?
ROMEO: The exchange of thy love's faithful vow for mine.
JULIET: I gave thee mine before thou didst request it;
        And yet I would it were to give again.
130 **ROMEO:** Wouldst thou withdraw it? For what purpose, love?
JULIET: But to be frank, and give it thee again.
        And yet I wish but for the thing I have.
        My bounty is as boundless as the sea,
        My love as deep; the more I give to thee,
135   The more I have, for both are infinite.

NURSE *calls within.*

        I hear some noise within. Dear love, adieu!
        Anon, good nurse! Sweet Montague, be true.
        Stay but a little, I will come again.

Exit, above.

ROMEO: O blessèd, blessèd night! I am afeard,
140   Being in night, all this is but a dream,
        Too flattering-sweet to be substantial.

Re-enter JULIET, *above.*

JULIET: Three words, dear Romeo, and good night indeed.
        If that thy bent of love be honourable,
        Thy purpose marriage, send me word tomorrow,
145   By one that I'll procure to come to thee,

146 *rite:* ceremony

147 *fortunes:* destiny

151 *by and by:* immediately

152 *cease:* stop

strife: endeavour, effort

154 *so thrive my soul:* just as my soul may be saved (from being damned)

155 *thy light:* the light of your presence

157 *toward school with heavy looks:* so (do schoolboys go) to school looking unhappy

158 *hist!:* hey!

falconer: Falkner

159 *lure:* persuade to return

tassel-gentle: (männlicher) Wanderfalke

160 *bondage is hoarse:* being in my father's house makes me have to whisper

– Juliet does not feel free in her house. Aware of the difficult situation she is in, she must make sure that no one discovers her speaking to Romeo.

161 *else:* otherwise

Note, ll. 161–162: Echo was one of the nymphs visited by Zeus. When Zeus's wife, Hera, was looking for him, Echo detained her by talking to her non-stop. Hera condemned her to always repeat the last word of someone else's sentence, but never begin one. Punished in this way, she spent much of her time alone in caves.

166 *attending:* listening

167 *nyas* [ˈnaɪəs]: young hawk still in the nest

o'clock: time

176 *I would have thee gone:* I wish you would go

177 *wanton:* young naughty child

Where and what time thou wilt perform the rite;
And all my fortunes at thy foot I'll lay
And follow thee my lord throughout the world.

NURSE: *[Within]* Madam!

150 **JULIET:** I come, anon. – But if thou mean'st not well,
I do beseech thee –

NURSE: *[Within]* Madam!

JULIET: By and by, I come –
To cease thy strife, and leave me to my grief:
Tomorrow will I send.

ROMEO: So thrive my soul –

JULIET: A thousand times good night!

Exit, above.

155 **ROMEO:** A thousand times the worse, to want thy light.
Love goes toward love, as schoolboys from their books,
But love from love, toward school with heavy looks.

Retiring.

Re-enter JULIET, *above.*

JULIET: Hist! Romeo, hist! O, for a falconer's voice,
To lure this tassel-gentle back again!
160 Bondage is hoarse, and may not speak aloud;
Else would I tear the cave where Echo lies,
And make her airy tongue more hoarse than mine
With repetition of my Romeo's name.

ROMEO: It is my soul that calls upon my name.
165 How silver-sweet sound lovers' tongues by night,
Like softest music to attending ears!

JULIET: Romeo!

ROMEO: My nyas?

JULIET: What o'clock tomorrow
Shall I send to thee?

ROMEO: At the hour of nine.

JULIET: I will not fail: 'Tis twenty years till then.
170 I have forgot why I did call thee back.

ROMEO: Let me stand here till thou remember it.

JULIET: I shall forget, to have thee still stand there,
Remembering how I love thy company.

ROMEO: And I'll still stay, to have thee still forget,
175 Forgetting any other home but this.

JULIET: 'Tis almost morning. I would have thee gone;
And yet no further than a wanton's bird,
Who lets it hop a little from her hand,

179 *gyves* [dʒaɪvz]: chains
180 *plucks:* pulls suddenly
183 *cherishing:* loving care
185 *morrow:* tomorrow
186 *dwell:* live
187 *I would I were:* I wish I were
188 *ghostly:* spiritual
　　friar ['fraɪə]: Mönch
　　close: secluded; small
189 *crave:* seek
　　dear hap: good fortune

Like a poor prisoner in his twisted gyves,
180 And with a silk thread plucks it back again,
So loving-jealous of his liberty.

ROMEO: I would I were thy bird.

JULIET: Sweet, so would I.
Yet I should kill thee with much cherishing.
Good night, good night! Parting is such sweet sorrow,
185 That I shall say good night till it be morrow.

Exit above.

ROMEO: Sleep dwell upon thine eyes, peace in thy breast!
Would I were sleep and peace, so sweet to rest!
Hence will I to my ghostly friar's close cell,
His help to crave, and my dear hap to tell.

Exit.

1 In 4 groups, analyse these speeches and dialogues from the scene closely.

1. Romeo: ll. 1–32

2. Juliet and Romeo: ll. 33–57

3. Juliet: ll. 85–106

4. Juliet and Romeo: ll. 158–185

Use the following questions to guide your analysis:

– What do the speakers say about their beloved and their own feelings?

– What images do they use to express their feelings?

– What mood is created by these images?

2 Look at ll. 52–84 and ll. 107–135 and describe Juliet's and Romeo's characters from what you learn here.

3 State in your own words what plans are being discussed in ll. 142–148 (Juliet) and ll. 180–189 (Romeo). Comment on this development.

4 Discuss why this scene is one of the most famous dramatic scenes of all time.

Summary

Romeo and Juliet meet at Friar Laurence's cell so that they can get married.

Notes and annotations

1 *so smile the heavens:* may the heavens smile

2 so that afterwards we will not be punished with sorrow

3 *come what sorrow can:* no matter what sorrow may come

4 *countervail:* outweigh, be equal to

   the exchange of joy: the joy for which it will be taken in exchange for

6 *close our hands:* join our hands together

7 *do what he dare:* may do as he likes

Note, ll. 9–15: Friar Laurence warns about passion: he compares it first to the mixture of fire and gunpowder, which when they meet, cause a big flash but then there is nothing left. Then he compares it to the sweetness of honey which due to its taste may ruin a person's appetite.

9 *violent:* strong and passionate

10 *triumph:* the greatest point

   powder: gunpowder

11 *consume:* einander verbrauchen

12 *loathsome* ['laʊðsəm]: very unpleasant; hated

   his: its

13 *confounds:* destroys

14 *long love doth so:* a longlasting love will love like that (i.e. with moderation)

15 too quick can seem the same as late *(tardy)* being too slow

17 *everlasting:* that will last for a very long time

   flint: stone (of the floor)

18 *bestride:* walk along

   gossamer: thread of a spider's web

19 *idles* ['aɪdəlz]: floats

   wanton: pleasant, luxurious

20 *vanity:* the empty delights of the world; the pleasure of love

21 *good even:* good evening

23 I must give Romeo as much thanks as Romeo gave me, to even things out.

   – One can presume that Romeo just kissed her, and she now kisses him in return.

24 *measure:* measuring cup (used in cooking)

25 *heaped:* gehäuft

25–26 *and that thy skill ... blazon* ['bleɪzən] *it:* and if your skill for describing *(blazon)* it is greater

27 *neighbour:* surrounding

   rich music's tongue: the beautiful sound of your voice

28 *unfold:* express

29 *in either:* in each other

   encounter: meeting

Act II, Scene 6

Romeo persuades Friar Laurence to marry him and Juliet. The friar has his doubts about Romeo's feelings but thinks the marriage may heal their families' enmity.

Tybalt sends a challenge to Romeo. Mercutio and Benvolio joke around with Romeo until Juliet's nurse turns up to ask him about his plans for the marriage.

Juliet waits impatiently for her Nurse's return. When she does return, however, she teases Juliet by not revealing immediately what Romeo had to say. She then tells Juliet that she must go to Friar Laurence, where Romeo is waiting to get married to her.

Friar Laurence's cell.

Enter FRIAR LAURENCE *and* ROMEO.

FRIAR LAURENCE: So smile the heavens upon this holy act,
    That after hours with sorrow chide us not!
ROMEO: Amen, amen! But come what sorrow can,
    It cannot countervail the exchange of joy
5   That one short minute gives me in her sight:
    Do thou but close our hands with holy words,
    Then love-devouring death do what he dare;
    It is enough I may but call her mine.
FRIAR LAURENCE: These violent delights have violent ends
10   And in their triumph die, like fire and powder,
    Which, as they kiss, consume: the sweetest honey
    Is loathsome in his own deliciousness
    And in the taste confounds the appetite.
    Therefore love moderately; long love doth so;
15   Too swift arrives as tardy as too slow.

Enter JULIET.

    Here comes the lady: O, so light a foot
    Will ne'er wear out the everlasting flint.
    A lover may bestride the gossamer
    That idles in the wanton summer air,
20   And yet not fall; so light is vanity.
JULIET: Good even to my ghostly cònfessor.
FRIAR LAURENCE: Romeo shall thank thee, daughter, for us both.
JULIET: As much to him, else is his thanks too much.
ROMEO: Ah, Juliet, if the measure of thy joy
25   Be heaped like mine and that thy skill be more
    To blazon it, then sweeten with thy breath
    This neighbour air, and let rich music's tongue
    Unfold the imagined happiness that both
    Receive in either by this dear encounter.

30 *conceit:* imagination

    matter: real substance

31 *brags of:* boasts of, takes pride in

    ornament: decoration; appearances

32 Those who can count their money *(worth)* are little more than beggars

34 *sum up sum:* add up the total amount

35 *make short work:* do the ceremony quickly

36 *stay alone:* be alone with each other

37 *incorporate:* make one flesh of; join together

30   **JULIET:** Conceit, more rich in matter than in words,
    Brags of his substance, not of ornament.
    They are but beggars that can count their worth;
    But my true love is grown to such excess
    I cannot sum up sum of half my wealth.
35   **FRIAR LAURENCE:** Come, come with me, and we will make short work;
    For, by your leaves, you shall not stay alone
    Till holy church incorporate two in one.

Exeunt.

1   True or False

Read the text and decide if the characters say the following:

T   F

☐   ☐   Romeo: I am so happy to be married to Juliet that afterwards I don't care if I die.

☐   ☐   Friar Laurence: Strong passions lead to good marriages.

☐   ☐   Friar Laurence: Don't overdo your passion as it may die due to excess.

☐   ☐   Friar Laurence: If you love moderately, you will swiftly get bored.

☐   ☐   Romeo: Juliet, if you love me as I love you, we will be happy.

☐   ☐   Juliet: I am rich and in love.

☐   ☐   Friar Laurence: You can only spend the night together once you are married.

2   Examine the dialogue between the friar and Romeo (ll. 1–15), paying particular attention to contrasts in their imagery. Explain these contrasts, and state what they signify for the whole of the story.

Looking back on Act II

3   Imagine the Nurse tells a friend her news with regard to Juliet and Romeo. Write the conversation.

4   A girl in Juliet's position or a young man in Romeo's position in our days tells a friend about her or his falling in love. Write either a dialogue (face to face or on the telephone) or an e-mail message from that person's point of view.

Summary

Tybalt wants to fight with Romeo, but Romeo refuses to be provoked. Mercutio, however, provokes Tybalt to fight with him and is killed. Romeo then avenges Mercutio by killing Tybalt.

Notes and annotations

1 *my man:* the person I am looking for

   – Mercutio twists the meaning in the next line to 'my man servant'.

2 *wear:* wears

   – 'wear' is the subjunctive form. Today the forms 'wore' or 'were to wear' would be correct.

   livery: uniform worn by servants to indicate they belong to a certain family

3 *go before to field:* go to the duelling field

   follower: attendant

4 *your worship:* form of address to high-born noble (here, used mockingly)

5 *the hate I bear thee:* the hate which I feel towards you

   afford: allow

8 *excuse:* mildern

8–9 *the appertaining rage to such a greeting:* the appropriate anger at being greeted with such an insult

14 *devise:* imagine

16 *tender:* value

19 *alla stoccata:* at the thrust

   – Mercutio is referring to Tybalt, who he had previously mocked for his duelling skills.

   carries it away: wins

Note, ll. 20, 22: Tybalt was the name of the Prince of Cats in the medieval fable 'Reynard the Fox'.

20 *walk:* go away to fight a duel

Note, l. 22: In England cats are traditionally said to have nine lives.

23 *make bold withal:* do as I please with

   as you shall use me hereafter: depending on how you treat me from now on

   dry-beat: whip without drawing blood

24 *pilcher:* Schwertscheide

   ears: Griff

25 *ere:* before

28 *passado:* type of sword movement

30 *forbear:* stop

Act III, Scene 1 (extracts)

Mercutio and Benvolio and some servants are in a public place fooling around. Tybalt and other Capulets enter. Tybalt asks about Romeo, as he has challenged him and received no answer.

A public place.

MERCUTIO, BENVOLIO *and* TYBALT, *page and servants. Enter* ROMEO.

TYBALT: Well, peace be with you, sir: here comes my man.

MERCUTIO: But I'll be hanged, sir, if he wear your livery:
Marry, go before to field, he'll be your follower.
Your worship in that sense may call him 'man'.

5   TYBALT: Romeo, the hate I bear thee can afford
No better term than this: thou art a villain.

ROMEO: Tybalt, the reason that I have to love thee
Doth much excuse the appertaining rage
To such a greeting. Villain am I none;

10   Therefore farewell, I see thou know'st me not.

TYBALT: Boy, this shall not excuse the injuries
That thou hast done me; therefore turn and draw.

ROMEO: I do protest, I never injured thee,
But love thee better than thou canst devise,

15   Till thou shalt know the reason of my love.
And so, good Capulet, which name I tender
As dearly as my own, be satisfied.

MERCUTIO: O calm, dishonourable, vile submission!
'Alla stoccata' carries it away.

Draws.

20   Tybalt, you rat-catcher, will you walk?

TYBALT: What wouldst thou have with me?

MERCUTIO: Good king of cats, nothing but one of your nine lives that I mean
to make bold withal, and as you shall use me hereafter, dry-beat the rest of
the eight. Will you pluck your sword out of his pilcher by the ears? Make

25   haste, lest mine be about your ears ere it be out.

TYBALT: I am for you.

Drawing.

ROMEO: Gentle Mercutio, put thy rapier up.

MERCUTIO: Come, sir, your 'passado'.

They fight.

ROMEO: Draw, Benvolio; beat down their weapons.

30   Gentlemen, for shame, forbear this outrage!
Tybalt, Mercutio, the prince expressly hath

32 *bandying:* fighting

• *flies:* escapes

34 *o':* on

sped: killed

35 *hath nothing:* has no injuries

37 *villain:* (here) a person of low social status

39 *well:* Brunnen

40 *'twill serve:* it will be enough to kill me

Note, l. 40: Even in death Mercutio puns. Here, he uses 'grave man' as in 'serious man' but also 'a man in the grave'.

41 *peppered:* finished

43 *braggart, rogue, villain:* terms of insults

by the book of arithmetic: according to the rules of fencing (i.e. with no imagination)

Forbidden bandying in Verona streets:
Hold, Tybalt! Good Mercutio!

TYBALT *under* ROMEO'S *arm stabs* MERCUTIO, *and flies with his followers.*

MERCUTIO: I am hurt.
    A plague o' both houses! I am sped.
35 Is he gone, and hath nothing?
    BENVOLIO: What, art thou hurt?
    MERCUTIO: Ay, ay, a scratch, a scratch; marry, 'tis enough.
    Where is my page? Go, villain, fetch a surgeon.

Exit Page.

ROMEO: Courage, man; the hurt cannot be much.
    MERCUTIO: No, 'tis not so deep as a well, nor so wide as a church-door; but 'tis
40 enough, 'twill serve: ask for me tomorrow, and you shall find me a grave
    man. I am peppered, I warrant, for this world. A plague o' both your
    houses! 'Zounds, a dog, a rat, a mouse, a cat, to scratch a man to death! A
    braggart, a rogue, a villain, that fights by the book of arithmetic! Why the
    devil came you between us? I was hurt under your arm.
45 ROMEO: I thought all for the best.
    MERCUTIO: Help me into some house, Benvolio,
    Or I shall faint. A plague o' both your houses!

48–49 *I have it, and soundly too:* I have been fatally wounded and of that there is no doubt

50 *near ally:* close relative

51 *very:* true

　mortal hurt: fatal wound

52 *in my behalf:* due to me, instead of me

53 *slander:* insults

54 *kinsman:* relative

56 *temper:* character

　softened valour's steel: weakened my courage

58 *gallant:* brave

　aspired: gone up to

59 *untimely:* prematurely

　scorn the earth: be angry at the earth, i.e. decide to leave this world

60–61 the terrible event of today will hang over future days; this begins the misery that other days must bring to an end.

63 *slain:* killed

64 *respective lenity:* gentleness/mercy which respects the fact that Tybalt is now a relative

65 *fire-eyed:* having eyes that glow with fire

　fury: anger

　conduct: guide

67 *late:* just now

69 *staying:* waiting

71 *wretched* ['retʃɪd]: worthless

　consort: accompany

72 *this:* this sword

　determine: decide

74 *up:* aroused, angry

75 *amazed:* shocked, confused

　doom thee: condemn you to

Note, l. 77: Romeo calls himself fortune's fool (a fool was an entertainer in a wealthy household), because fortune seems to be playing with him for her entertainment, first giving him love and happiness and now making him a murderer and criminal.

They have made worms' meat of me. I have it,
And soundly too. Your houses!

Exeunt MERCUTIO *and* BENVOLIO.

50 **ROMEO:** This gentleman, the prince's near ally,
My very friend, hath got his mortal hurt
In my behalf; my reputation stained
With Tybalt's slander – Tybalt, that an hour
Hath been my kinsman! O sweet Juliet,
55 Thy beauty hath made me effeminate
And in my temper softened valour's steel!

Re-enter BENVOLIO.

BENVOLIO: O Romeo, Romeo, brave Mercutio's dead!
That gallant spirit hath aspired the clouds,
Which too untimely here did scorn the earth.
60 **ROMEO:** This day's black fate on more days doth depend;
This but begins the woe others must end.
BENVOLIO: Here comes the furious Tybalt back again.
ROMEO: Alive, in triumph! and Mercutio slain!
Away to heaven, respective lenity,
65 And fire-eyed fury be my conduct now!

Re-enter TYBALT.

Now, Tybalt, take the 'villain' back again,
That late thou gavest me; for Mercutio's soul
Is but a little way above our heads,
Staying for thine to keep him company:
70 Either thou, or I, or both, must go with him.
TYBALT: Thou, wretched boy, that didst consort him here,
Shalt with him hence.
ROMEO: This shall determine that.

They fight; TYBALT *falls.*

BENVOLIO: Romeo, away, be gone!
The citizens are up, and Tybalt slain.
75 Stand not amazed. The prince will doom thee death,
If thou art taken. Hence, be gone, away!
ROMEO: O, I am fortune's fool!
BENVOLIO: Why dost thou stay?

Exit ROMEO.

The Prince then finds out about the fight and exiles Romeo from Verona.

INFOBOX — Dramatic structure

According to classical dramatic theory, a play is divided into five distinctive sections. Modern dramas do not follow this structure any more, but in Shakespeare's plays they are still relevant to understand the pattern of the plot. The action starts with the **exposition** or introduction, which presents the protagonists and the main plot and is then driven forward by the **inciting moment**, i.e. an event which leads to a conflict or problem that needs to be solved during the play. Further conflicts complicate the plot and the characters meet more obstacles in the next phase, the **rising action**. The highest point of tension is reached with the **climax** or turning-point, which marks a complete change for the protagonist for the better (in a comedy) or worse (in a tragedy). The following phase is called the **falling action**, which is usually shorter than the rising action, and contains developments leading to the **resolution** (in a comedy) or the **catastrophe** (in a tragedy) that end the play.

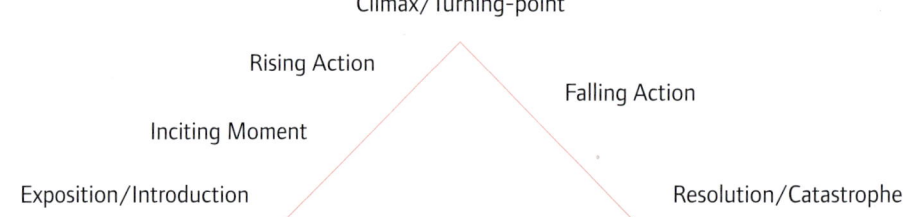

Climax/Turning-point

Rising Action

Falling Action

Inciting Moment

Exposition/Introduction

Resolution/Catastrophe

1 **Listing**

Outline the steps that lead to the death of Tybalt.

Step 1: _____

Step 2: _____

Step 3: _____

Step 4: _____

Step 5: _____

Step 6: _____

Step 7: _____ ...

2 Analyse Romeo's behaviour and its consequences for others as well as for himself.

3 Look at the 'Infobox: Dramatic structure' (p. 52). Explain which part of the play is the exposition and which event is the inciting moment.

Summary

When Juliet learns that it was Romeo who killed her beloved cousin Tybalt, she is at first confused. However, her love for her new husband is stronger than all else, so the Nurse promises to go and find Romeo at Friar Laurence's cell and tell him to come to Juliet before he goes into exile.

Notes and annotations

3 *shed:* vergießen

5 *serpent:* snake

  hid with: hidden behind

  a flowering face: a face that looks like a flower

6 *dragon:* Drache

  keep: live in

7 *fiend* [fiːnd]: devil

8 *raven* ['reɪvən]: Rabe

  wolvish-ravening ['rævənɪŋ]: having the appetite of a wolf

9 hated reality with a heavenly appearance

10 *just:* exact

  justly seem'st: truly appear

13 *bower* [baʊə]: enclose

Note, ll. 13–14: Juliet is referring to the serpent that tempted Eve in the Garden of Eden *(mortal paradise)*.

15 *vile matter:* nasty content

18 *perjured:* liars

19 *forsworn:* not able to keep promises

  naught [nɔːt]: nothing; wicked, evil

  dissemblers: Heuchler

20 *aqua vitae:* Branntwein

22 *blistered be …:* may … be full of blisters (= Blasen)

27 *chide at:* be angry with

30 *poor my lord:* my poor lord

  smooth: speak well of

31 *three-hours wife:* wife of three hours

  mangled: damaged

34 *native spring:* eyes

35 *tributary drops:* tears (= Tränen) which pay a tribute

  woe: deep sadness

36 which you are offering up mistakenly for a joyful occasion

  – Juliet has suddenly realized she should not be crying as her husband is alive.

37 *that:* who

INFOBOX	**Oxymoron**

An oxymoron (plural: oxymora or oxymorons) is a figure of speech that combines two contradictory terms. The most common form consists of an adjective-noun combination.

Act III, Scene 2

Juliet is waiting impatiently for the Nurse to come with ropes so that Romeo can secretly climb up to her room that night. The Nurse, however, brings her the bad news of the fight. At first Juliet understands that Romeo has been killed, as the Nurse is too upset to explain properly, but finally she tells Juliet what has happened.

NURSE: Tybalt is gone, and Romeo banished.
   Romeo that killed him, he is banished.
JULIET: O God! Did Romeo's hand shed Tybalt's blood?
NURSE: It did, it did. Alas the day, it did!
5 JULIET: O serpent heart, hid with a flowering face!
   Did ever dragon keep so fair a cave?
   Beautiful tyrant! Fiend angelical!
   Dove-feathered raven! Wolvish-ravening lamb!
   Despisèd substance of divinest show!
10   Just opposite to what thou justly seem'st,
   A damnèd saint, an honourable villain!
   O nature, what hadst thou to do in hell,
   When thou didst bower the spirit of a fiend
   In mortal paradise of such sweet flesh?
15   Was ever book containing such vile matter
   So fairly bound? O that deceit should dwell
   In such a gorgeous palace!
NURSE: There's no trust,
   No faith, no honesty in men. All perjured,
   All forsworn, all naught, all dissemblers.
20   Ah, where's my man? Give me some aqua vitae.
   These griefs, these woes, these sorrows make me old.
   Shame come to Romeo!
JULIET: Blistered be thy tongue
   For such a wish! He was not born to shame.
   Upon his brow shame is ashamed to sit;
25   For 'tis a throne where honour may be crowned
   Sole monarch of the universal earth.
   O, what a beast was I to chide at him!
NURSE: Will you speak well of him that killed your cousin?
JULIET: Shall I speak ill of him that is my husband?
30   Ah, poor my lord, what tongue shall smooth thy name,
   When I, thy three-hours wife, have mangled it?
   But wherefore, villain, didst thou kill my cousin?
   That villain cousin would have killed my husband.
   Back, foolish tears, back to your native spring;
35   Your tributary drops belong to woe,
   Which you, mistaking, offer up to joy.
   My husband lives, that Tybalt would have slain;

40 *worser:* worse

41 *fain:* gladly

43 *deeds:* actions

    sinners: Sünder

45–46 *that one word … Tybalts:* that one word 'banished' is as bad as ten thousand Tybalts dead

48–49 or if sorrow loves to have company and needs to be joined with other sorrows

51 *nay:* no

52 which might have caused *(moved)* ordinary *(modern)* grief *(lamentations)*

53 *rear-ward:* Nachhutgefecht

54 *word:* sentence, phrase

58 *in that word's death:* in the death which that word causes

    sound: express

60 *wail:* Klagelaute von sich geben

    corse: dead body

61 *thither:* dahin

62 *spent:* aufgebraucht

64 *beguiled:* deceived, cheated

65 *for:* as

66 *highway:* path

67 *maid:* virgin

    maiden-widowed: a virgin and a widow

69 *maidenhead:* Jungfernhäutchen

70 *hie* [haɪ]: go quickly

    chamber: room

71 *wot:* know

72 *hark ye:* listen

73 *is hid:* is hiding

74 *knight:* Ritter

And Tybalt's dead, that would have slain my husband:
All this is comfort. Wherefore weep I then?
40   Some word there was, worser than Tybalt's death,
That murdered me; I would forget it fain,
But, O, it presses to my memory,
Like damnèd guilty deeds to sinners' minds:
'Tybalt is dead, and Romeo – banishèd';
45   That 'banishèd,' that one word 'banishèd,'
Hath slain ten thousand Tybalts. Tybalt's death
Was woe enough, if it had ended there;
Or, if sour woe delights in fellowship
And needly will be ranked with other griefs,
50   Why followed not, when she said 'Tybalt's dead,'
Thy father, or thy mother, nay, or both,
Which modern lamentations might have moved?
But with a rear-ward following Tybalt's death,
'Romeo is banishèd': to speak that word,
55   Is father, mother, Tybalt, Romeo, Juliet,
All slain, all dead. 'Romeo is banishèd!'
There is no end, no limit, measure, bound,
In that word's death; no words can that woe sound.
Where is my father and my mother, nurse?
60   **NURSE:** Weeping and wailing over Tybalt's corse.
Will you go to them? I will bring you thither.
JULIET: Wash they his wounds with tears? Mine shall be spent,
When theirs are dry, for Romeo's banishment.
Take up those cords. Poor ropes, you are beguiled,
65   Both you and I, for Romeo is exiled.
He made you for a highway to my bed;
But I, a maid, die maiden-widowèd.
Come, cords, come, nurse. I'll to my wedding-bed;
And death, not Romeo, take my maidenhead!
70   **NURSE:** Hie to your chamber. I'll find Romeo
To comfort you. I wot well where he is.
Hark ye, your Romeo will be here at night.
I'll to him. He is hid at Laurence' cell.
JULIET: O, find him! Give this ring to my true knight,
75   And bid him come to take his last farewell.

Exeunt.

INFOBOX   **William Shakespeare**

William Shakespeare (1564–1616) is widely regarded as the greatest writer in the English language. His surviving work consists of about 38 plays, 154 sonnets and several other poems. His plays are performed worldwide more often than those of any other playwright.

We know little about Shakespeare. He was born and brought up in Stratford-upon-Avon. His father was a member of the town council and a maker of gloves. At the age of 18, he married Anne Hathaway, with whom he had three children: Susanna (born 1583), and twins Hamnet and Judith (born 1585). At some point he moved to London, where by 1592 he had become known as a playwright and was beginning his acting career in the theatres of London. In 1594 a group of actors, including Shakespeare, formed the Lord Chamberlain's Men, which soon became the leading company in London. In 1599, they built their own theatre on the south bank of the River Thames, called the Globe. In 1608 the company also took over the Blackfriars indoor theatre. Records of Shakespeare's property purchases and investments indicate that the company made him a wealthy man. After the death of Queen Elizabeth in 1603, the company was awarded a royal patent by King James I, and changed its name to the King's Men.

He appears to have retired to Stratford around 1613 at the age of 49, where he died three years later. Few records of Shakespeare's private life survive, and there has been considerable speculation about such matters as his physical appearance, sexuality, religious beliefs, and whether the works attributed to him were written by others.

Shakespeare produced most of his known work between 1589 and 1613. His early plays were mainly comedies and histories (the latter concerned the history of England in the Middle Ages). Until about 1608 he wrote mainly tragedies, including *Hamlet, King Lear, Othello* and *Macbeth*. In his last phase, he wrote romances, such as *The Tempest. Romeo and Juliet* is believed to have been written between 1591 and 1595. While many of his plays were published in editions of varying quality and accuracy during his lifetime, in 1623, two of his former colleagues published the First Folio, a collected edition of his dramatic works that included all but two of the plays now recognised as Shakespeare's. His sonnets were published in 1609.

1 **True or False**

Decide which of the following is true and which false:

T F

☐ ☐ Juliet is relieved that Romeo is alive, as she cares more for him than Tybalt.

☐ ☐ Juliet is first angry with Romeo, then decides he acted in good faith.

☐ ☐ Juliet is upset as she does not know if Romeo is alive, dead or banished.

☐ ☐ Juliet decides to carry on being a faithful wife because the Nurse persuades her that this is for the best.

2 Examine the images Juliet uses when she hears of what has happened and explain how they are related to each other (cf. 'Infobox: Oxymoron', p. 54).

3 Explain why Juliet despairs at the sight of the ropes that the Nurse has brought (ll. 62–69), and comment on the fact that these lines rhyme as opposed to most others spoken in the scene.

Summary

Just before dawn Romeo reluctantly leaves Juliet after they have spent the night together.

Notes and annotations

2 *nightingale:* Nachtigall

lark: Lerche

– The nightingale is one of the few birds that sings at night; only the male nightingale sings, not the female one as stated here (cf. 'she', l. 4). The lark, like most birds, starts singing early in the morning. It also sings when it is in flight (cf. ll. 21–22).

3 *pierced:* broke through

fearful: full of fear

hollow: empty space

4 *yon:* over there

pomegranate: Granatapfel

6 *herald:* person who announces sth.

morn: morning

7 *envious:* neidisch

streaks: Streifen

8 *lace:* säumen, umwinden

severing: which are parting

yonder: over there

9 *night's candles:* the stars

jocund: cheerful, happy

10 *tiptoe:* auf Zehenspitzen

misty: nebelig

12 *ay:* indeed

Note, l. 13: Meteors were believed to come from (*exhale:* ausstoßen) the sun.

17 *ta'en* [teɪn]: taken, captured, arrested

18 *so thou will have it so:* if that is what you want

20 *reflex:* reflection

Cynthia: another name for Diana, goddess of the moon, due to her birthplace on Mount Cynthus

brow: face

21 *nor that is not:* nor is that

notes: Gesang

22 *vaulty:* gewölbt

23 *care:* desire

will: Willenskraft

24 *wills:* wants

26 *hie hence* [haɪ] : go from here

28 *straining:* forcing out of its mouth

harsh discords: rough noises

unpleasing sharps: high notes that are unpleasant

29 *sweet division:* enjoyable melodic music

– There is a pun on division (= separation).

Act III, Scene 5

In Act III, Scene 3, Romeo is very upset by the news of his banishment. Friar Laurence tries to comfort him. The Nurse brings news that Juliet is just as miserable as Romeo. Friar Laurence tells Romeo to go to Juliet, then to Mantua where he should remain until the Prince can be persuaded to pardon him.
In Act III, Scene 4, Capulet promises Paris that Juliet will marry him later that same week.

Capulet's orchard.

Enter ROMEO *and* JULIET *above, at the window.*

JULIET: Wilt thou be gone? It is not yet near day.
　　　It was the nightingale, and not the lark,
　　　That pierced the fearful hollow of thine ear.
　　　Nightly she sings on yon pomegranate tree.
5　　　Believe me, love, it was the nightingale.
ROMEO: It was the lark, the herald of the morn,
　　　No nightingale. Look, love, what envious streaks
　　　Do lace the severing clouds in yonder east.
　　　Night's candles are burnt out, and jocund day
10　　Stands tiptoe on the misty mountain tops.
　　　I must be gone and live, or stay and die.
JULIET: Yon light is not daylight, I know it, ay.
　　　It is some meteor that the sun exhales,
　　　To be to thee this night a torch-bearer,
15　　And light thee on thy way to Mantua.
　　　Therefore stay yet; thou need'st not to be gone.
ROMEO: Let me be ta'en, let me be put to death;
　　　I am content, so thou wilt have it so.
　　　I'll say yon grey is not the morning's eye,
20　　'Tis but the pale reflex of Cynthia's brow;
　　　Nor that is not the lark, whose notes do beat
　　　The vaulty heaven so high above our heads.
　　　I have more care to stay than will to go.
　　　Come, death, and welcome! Juliet wills it so.
25　　How is't, my soul? Let's talk; it is not day.
JULIET: It is, it is! Hie hence, be gone, away!
　　　It is the lark that sings so out of tune,
　　　Straining harsh discords and unpleasing sharps.
　　　Some say the lark makes sweet division.
30　　This doth not so, for she divideth us.

31 *loathed:* hated

Note, ll. 31–33: It was said that the lark and toad (= Kröte) had exchanged *(changed)* eyes, as the lark was supposed to have ugly eyes, while the toad had attractive eyes. Juliet wishes they had exchanged voices, too, because the toad's ugly voice would help frighten *(affray)* them away from each other *(arm from arm)*.

34 *hunting:* chasing

hunt's-up: horn-blowing to wake up hunters (or newly married couples)

40 *broke:* angebrochen

be wary, look about: take care, watch out

45 for each minute seems as if it is many days long

46 *count:* way of reckoning

much in years: very old

47 *behold:* see

52–53 *these woes shall serve for sweet discourses:* we will talk lovingly about the troubles we had

54 *ill-divining:* that sees bad fortune ahead

55 *methinks:* I think

59 *dry:* thirsty

– It was thought that sorrow dried up the blood, so Romeo is saying they are pale from the lack of blood caused by the sorrow of their parting.

60 *fickle:* changing often and suddenly

61 *what doest thou:* why are you playing around

Some say the lark and loathèd toad changed eyes;
O, now I would they had changed voices too!
Since arm from arm that voice doth us affray,
Hunting thee hence with hunt's-up to the day,
35   O, now be gone! More light and light it grows.
ROMEO: More light and light; more dark and dark our woes!

Enter NURSE, *to the chamber.*

NURSE: Madam!
JULIET: Nurse?
NURSE: Your lady mother is coming to your chamber.
40   The day is broke; be wary, look about.

Exit.

JULIET: Then, window, let day in, and let life out.
ROMEO: Farewell, farewell! One kiss, and I'll descend.

He goeth down.

JULIET: Art thou gone so? Love, lord, ay, husband, friend!
I must hear from thee every day in the hour,
45   For in a minute there are many days.
O, by this count I shall be much in years
Ere I again behold my Romeo!
ROMEO: Farewell!
I will omit no opportunity
50   That may convey my greetings, love, to thee.
JULIET: O think'st thou we shall ever meet again?
ROMEO: I doubt it not; and all these woes shall serve
For sweet discourses in our time to come.
JULIET: O God, I have an ill-divining soul!
55   Methinks I see thee, now thou art so low,
As one dead in the bottom of a tomb.
Either my eyesight fails, or thou look'st pale.
ROMEO: And trust me, love, in my eye so do you.
Dry sorrow drinks our blood. Adieu, adieu!

Exit.

60   **JULIET:** O fortune, fortune! All men call thee fickle.
If thou art fickle, what dost thou with him
That is renowned for faith? Be fickle, fortune;
For then, I hope, thou wilt not keep him long,
But send him back.

Lady Capulet enters the room and informs Juliet that she is to be married to Paris. Juliet declares that she will not marry him. When Capulet hears of Juliet's refusal, he becomes enraged and threatens to throw her out of his house if she does not marry Paris.

1   Outline what the two lovers speak about before Romeo finally leaves Juliet.

2   Analyse their final dialogue (ll. 51–59) and comment on how it foreshadows future developments.

Looking back on Act III

3   Examine how the two strands of the plot – love and family feud – come to a climax in Act III.

4   Choose one of the following:

   a) Evaluate Juliet's present situation and her future prospects.

   b) Write a modern-English interior monologue from Juliet's point of view.

Summary

Friar Laurence gives Juliet a drug which will make her appear dead, so that the wedding to Paris will be called off and Romeo can come and take her to Mantua.

Notes and annotations

1 *merry:* happy, cheerful

  give consent: agree

3 *look:* make sure

  lie: sleep

5 *vial* ['vaɪl]: small bottle

6 *distilling liquor:* liquid which penetrates the entire body

  off: completely; all of it

7 *presently:* shortly afterwards

8 *drowsy:* that makes you want to sleep

  humour: feeling

  for: as

9 *native progress:* natural flow

  surcease: stop

10 *testify:* indicate

12 *paly:* pale

  eyes' windows: eyelids

14 *part:* part of the body

  supple government: power of movement

16 *borrowed likeness:* false similarity

  shrunk death: death that is not really death

21 *manner:* tradition, custom

22 *uncovered:* with your face uncovered

  bier: moveable stand on which a corpse is laid

23 *borne:* carried

  vault: Gruft

24 *kindred:* family

25 *against:* ready for the time when

26 *drift:* plan

31 *inconstant toy:* unbeständige Laune

32 weaken your bravery in carrying through with it (= the plan)

Act IV, Scene 1 (extracts)

Paris discusses the wedding with Friar Laurence. Juliet appears and behaves indifferently to Paris. When Paris has left, Juliet threatens that she will kill herself rather than marry Paris.

Friar Laurence's cell.

FRIAR LAURENCE *and* JULIET.

FRIAR LAURENCE: Hold, then. Go home, be merry, give consent
  To marry Paris. Wednesday is tomorrow.
  Tomorrow night look that thou lie alone.
  Let not thy nurse lie with thee in thy chamber.
5 Take thou this vial, being then in bed,
  And this distilling liquor drink thou off,
  When presently through all thy veins shall run
  A cold and drowsy humour, for no pulse
  Shall keep his native progress, but surcease.
10 No warmth, no breath, shall testify thou livest.
  The roses in thy lips and cheeks shall fade
  To paly ashes; thy eyes' windows fall,
  Like Death, when he shuts up the day of life.
  Each part, deprived of supple government,
15 Shall, stiff and stark and cold, appear like death;
  And in this borrowed likeness of shrunk death
  Thou shalt continue two and forty hours,
  And then awake as from a pleasant sleep.
  Now, when the bridegroom in the morning comes
20 To rouse thee from thy bed, there art thou dead.
  Then, as the manner of our country is,
  In thy best robes uncovered on the bier
  Thou shalt be borne to that same ancient vault
  Where all the kindred of the Capulets lie.
25 In the meantime, against thou shalt awake,
  Shall Romeo by my letters know our drift,
  And hither shall he come; and he and I
  Will watch thy waking, and that very night
  Shall Romeo bear thee hence to Mantua.
30 And this shall free thee from this present shame.
  If no inconstant toy, nor womanish fear,
  Abate thy valour in the acting it.

34 *hold:* take it (= the vial)
   prosperous: successful
35 *resolve:* Entschluss
37 *help afford:* provide help

JULIET: Give me, give me! O, tell not me of fear!

FRIAR LAURENCE: Hold. Get you gone, be strong and prosperous

35   In this resolve. I'll send a friar with speed

To Mantua, with my letters to thy lord.

JULIET: Love give me strength, and strength shall help afford.

Farewell, dear father!

Exeunt.

1 Rewrite in modern English what the Friar tells Juliet about the effects of the drug (ll. 5–32).

2 Study the imagery used in connection with Juliet's body on the one hand, and death on the other. Identify individual images and explain their effect.

3 Comment on Juliet's fearlessness regarding the Friar's dangerous plan (l. 33).

Summary

When she is finally alone in her room Juliet expresses her fears. She then takes the Friar's drug.

Notes and annotations

  1 *attires:* clothes

  3 *orisons:* prayers

  5 *cross:* contrary to what it should be

  7 *culled:* picked out, chosen

      necessaries: clothes that need to be worn

  8 *behoveful:* appropriate, needed

15 *a faint cold fear:* a fear that causes faintness (= Ohnmachtsgefühl) and cold

      thrills through: goes shivering through

19 *dismal:* awful, dreadful, terrible

      scene: action

      I needs must act: I have to do

23 *this:* her dagger

25 *subtly:* secretly

      ministered: provided

26 *lest:* in case

29 *still been tried:* always been proved by experience to be

30 *how:* what

Act IV, Scene 3

Juliet informs her parents that she will indeed marry Paris. Capulet is so relieved that he decides the marriage will take place the very next day. Juliet then goes to her room.

Juliet's chamber.

Enter JULIET *and* NURSE.

JULIET: Ay, those attires are best: but, gentle nurse,
    I pray thee, leave me to myself tonight;
    For I have need of many orisons
    To move the heavens to smile upon my state,
5   Which, well thou know'st, is cross, and full of sin.

Enter LADY CAPULET.

LADY CAPULET: What, are you busy, ho? Need you my help?
JULIET: No, madam. We have culled such necessaries
    As are behoveful for our state tomorrow.
    So please you, let me now be left alone,
10   And let the nurse this night sit up with you;
    For, I am sure, you have your hands full all,
    In this so sudden business.
LADY CAPULET: Good night.
    Get thee to bed, and rest; for thou hast need.

Exeunt LADY CAPULET *and* NURSE.

JULIET: Farewell! God knows when we shall meet again.
15   I have a faint cold fear thrills through my veins,
    That almost freezes up the heat of life.
    I'll call them back again to comfort me. –
    Nurse! – What should she do here?
    My dismal scene I needs must act alone.
20   Come, vial.
    What if this mixture do not work at all?
    Shall I be married then tomorrow morning?
    No, no; this shall forbid it: lie thou there.

Laying down her dagger.

    What if it be a poison, which the friar
25   Subtly hath ministered to have me dead,
    Lest in this marriage he should be dishonoured,
    Because he married me before to Romeo?
    I fear it is; and yet, methinks, it should not,
    For he hath still been tried a holy man.
30   How if, when I am laid into the tomb,
    I wake before the time that Romeo

32 *redeem:* save, rescue

33 *stifled:* unable to breathe

34 *mouth:* opening of the tomb

healthsome: healthy

35 *strangled:* erdrosselt

36 *like:* likely

37 *conceit:* thoughts, fantasy

39 *as:* as I will be

receptacle: place where corpses are received

42 *yet but green in earth:* just newly buried

43 *fester:* verrotten

shroud: cloth that covers a corpse

45 *alack:* expression of horror

is it not like that I: is it not possible that I

46 *loathsome* ['ləʊðsəm]: terrible, very unpleasant

47 *mandrake:* type of plant that was supposed to shriek when pulled out of the earth so that it drove people mad

48 *that:* so that

49 *distraught* [dɪ'strɔːt]: very frightened, terrified

50 *environed* [ɪn'vaɪrənd]: surrounded

51 *joints:* bones

52 *pluck:* pick up

mangled: verstümmelt

53 *rage:* madness

great: old, ancient

54 *dash out:* zerschmettern

Note, ll. 55–57: Juliet imagines seeing the ghost of Tybalt waiting for Romeo in the tomb.

56 *spit:* pierce

57 *rapier's point:* end of a sword

stay: stop

Note, stage directions: Curtains were first used around four-poster beds; only later were they used for windows. Here, one can presume that the bed was on the inner stage, where it could be concealed by curtains.

Come to redeem me? There's a fearful point!
Shall I not, then, be stifled in the vault,
To whose foul mouth no healthsome air breathes in,
35 And there die strangled ere my Romeo comes?
Or, if I live, is it not very like,
The horrible conceit of death and night,
Together with the terror of the place –
As in a vault, an ancient receptacle,
40 Where, for these many hundred years, the bones
Of all my buried ancestors are packed;
Where bloody Tybalt, yet but green in earth,
Lies festering in his shroud; where, as they say,
At some hours in the night spirits resort –
45 Alack, alack, is it not like that I,
So early waking – what with loathsome smells,
And shrieks like mandrakes torn out of the earth,
That living mortals, hearing them, run mad –
O, if I wake, shall I not be distraught,
50 Environèd with all these hideous fears?
And madly play with my forefather's joints?
And pluck the mangled Tybalt from his shroud?
And, in this rage, with some great kinsman's bone,
As with a club, dash out my desperate brains?
55 O, look! Methinks I see my cousin's ghost
Seeking out Romeo, that did spit his body
Upon a rapier's point. Stay, Tybalt, stay!
Romeo, I come! This do I drink to thee.

She falls upon her bed, within the curtains.

In the following scenes the Capulet household is preparing for the marriage.
Capulet sends the Nurse to get Juliet ready, who discovers her lifeless body in
her room. The whole family together with Paris mourn her death. Friar
Laurence tells them to stop weeping because Juliet is now in Heaven.

1 Describe the different fears Juliet expresses before taking the drug (ll. 21–58).

Looking back on Act IV

2 Discuss the dramatic function of Act IV considering that it is the fourth of five acts.
   (cf. also 'Infobox: Dramatic structure' on p. xx)

   – What questions are left open?

   – How is the tension maintained?

   – What is the overall mood of the act?

3 Write a short profile of Juliet based primarily on Act IV, comparing new sides of her character that
   came out in this act with how you perceived her in the previous acts.

Scene Summary

Romeo's servant Balthasar arrives in Mantua and tells Romeo that Juliet is dead. Romeo decides to go to Verona.

Notes and annotations

1 *the flattering truth of sleep:* dreams which seem truthful as they flatter (= schmeicheln) us

2 *presage* ['presɪdʒ]: hervorsagen

  at hand: nearby

Note, l. 3: This may be interpreted as 'my love' / 'Cupid' *(my bosom's lord)* sits lightly in Romeo's 'heart' *(throne)*, or as 'my heart' *(my bosom's lord)* sits lightly in Romeo's 'body' *(throne)*.

7 *leave to think:* the ability to think

10 *how sweet is love itself possessed:* how sweet it is to enjoy the reality of love

11 *but love's shadows:* even the dreams of love

  booted: wearing boots, to show that he has been travelling

15 *fares:* is doing

18 *Capel:* Capulet

  monument: tomb

20 *laid low:* buried, put to rest

21 *presently:* immediately

  took post: set out on horseback

  – Horses were changed at post-houses along the way, so that they would not be tired out too quickly. The horses were called 'post-horses'.

23 as it was you who gave me the duty of bringing you news

24 *defy:* widersetzen, trotzen

25 *lodging:* place where Romeo is staying

28–29 *import some misadventure:* indicate that some disaster may occur

29 *tush:* be quiet

  deceived: mistaken

33 *straight:* as soon as possible

Act V, Scene 1 (extracts)

Mantua. A street.

Enter ROMEO.

ROMEO: If I may trust the flattering truth of sleep,
My dreams presage some joyful news at hand.
My bosom's lord sits lightly in his throne;
And all this day an unaccustomed spirit

5   Lifts me above the ground with cheerful thoughts.
I dreamt my lady came and found me dead –
Strange dream that gives a dead man leave to think! –
And breathed such life with kisses in my lips,
That I revived, and was an emperor.

10   Ah me! How sweet is love itself possessed,
When but love's shadows are so rich in joy!

Enter BALTHASAR, *booted.*

News from Verona! – How now, Balthasar!
Dost thou not bring me letters from the friar?
How doth my lady? Is my father well?

15   How fares my Juliet? That I ask again,
For nothing can be ill, if she be well.
BALTHASAR: Then she is well, and nothing can be ill.
Her body sleeps in Capel's monument,
And her immortal part with angels lives.

20   I saw her laid low in her kindred's vault,
And presently took post to tell it you.
O, pardon me for bringing these ill news,
Since you did leave it for my office, sir.
ROMEO: Is it even so? Then I defy you, stars!

25   Thou know'st my lodging: get me ink and paper,
And hire post-horses; I will hence tonight.
BALTHASAR: I do beseech you, sir, have patience.
Your looks are pale and wild, and do import
Some misadventure.
ROMEO: Tush, thou art deceived.

30   Leave me, and do the thing I bid thee do.
Hast thou no letters to me from the friar?
BALTHASAR: No, my good lord.
ROMEO: No matter. Get thee gone,
And hire those horses. I'll be with thee straight.

Afterwards Romeo decides to go to Verona to see her corpse and then commit
suicide. He illegally buys a poison from a poor apothecary.

1 Point out the main elements of Romeo's dream and explain his interpretation of it (ll. 1–11).

2 Describe your mental image of the scene in a street in Mantua based on the excerpt alone: how do you 'see' Romeo before Balthasar's appearance, and how do you think his voice and posture change after the news?

Summary

Romeo sees Juliet, swallows his poison and dies. When Juliet wakes up, she discovers Romeo's body and stabs herself. Friar Laurence explains to the Prince and the two families how it all came to pass.

Note and annotations:

1   *oft:* often

2   *keeper:* prison warder, nurse

3   *lightning:* lightening (of mood/spirits)

7   *ensign:* Hoheitszeichen

8   *crimson:* dark red

Note, l. 9: Romeo describes Juliet's body as still being owned by beauty (as her body still has its red emblem), but death will soon conquer her body and raise (advance) its own pale flag.

12   *in twain:* entzwei

13   *sunder his:* end his (i.e. his youth)

16   *unsubstantial:* that has no body or form

17   *lean:* thin (as Death has no flesh)

    abhorred: hated

18   *paramour:* lover

20   *dim:* dark

22   *chambermaid:* personal maidservant

23   *set up my everlasting rest:* make my final decision to remain for ever

    – 'Set up your rest' is an expression from card playing, when a player asks for no more cards and is willing to bet on what he has in his hand. Romeo then plays with the expression 'everlasting rest' (= ewige Ruhe).

24   *shake the yoke:* break free from the oppression (*yoke:* Joch)

    inauspicious stars: misfortune

25   *your last:* for the last time

27   *seal:* besiegelt

    righteous ['raɪtʃəs]: tugendhaft

28   *dateless bargain:* contract that is unlimited

    engrossing: that takes/consumes everything

29   *conduct:* thing/person that leads/guides (i.e. the poison)

    unsavoury: having an unpleasant taste

31   *bark:* ship

32   *true:* trustworthy

Act V, Scene 3

A churchyard; in it a tomb belonging to the Capulets.

Friar Laurence discovers that his message to Romeo was not delivered as planned because his messenger was delayed. He hurries to the tomb to assist Juliet when she wakes up. Before he arrives, Paris visits Juliet's tomb, where later Romeo turns up. They fight, and Paris is killed.

Enter ROMEO.

ROMEO: How oft when men are at the point of death
Have they been merry, which their keepers call
A lightning before death. O, how may I
Call this a lightning? O my love! my wife!
5 Death, that hath sucked the honey of thy breath,
Hath had no power yet upon thy beauty.
Thou art not conquered: beauty's ensign yet
Is crimson in thy lips and in thy cheeks,
And death's pale flag is not advancèd there.
10 Tybalt, liest thou there in thy bloody sheet?
O, what more favour can I do to thee,
Than with that hand that cut thy youth in twain
To sunder his that was thine enemy?
Forgive me, cousin! Ah, dear Juliet,
15 Why art thou yet so fair? Shall I believe
That unsubstantial Death is amorous,
And that the lean abhorrèd monster keeps
Thee here in dark to be his paramour?
For fear of that, I still will stay with thee;
20 And never from this palace of dim night
Depart again. Here, here will I remain
With worms that are thy chambermaids. O, here
Will I set up my everlasting rest,
And shake the yoke of inauspicious stars
25 From this world-wearied flesh. Eyes, look your last!
Arms, take your last embrace! And, lips, O you
The doors of breath, seal with a righteous kiss
A dateless bargain to engrossing Death!
Come, bitter conduct, come, unsavoury guide!
30 Thou desperate pilot, now at once run on
The dashing rocks thy sea-sick weary bark!
Here's to my love!

Drinks.

                   O true apothecary!
Thy drugs are quick. Thus with a kiss I die.

- *crow:* Brecheisen, Brechstange
34 *Saint Francis be my speed:* may St Francis help me get there quickly
35 *stumbled:* fallen
37 *bliss:* Glückseligkeit
38 *vainly:* for no point whatsoever
39 *grub:* Made
   discern: can see, make out
45 *knows not but I am gone hence:* thinks that I have gone away
55 *what mean ...:* what does it mean that ... / why do ...
   masterless: that are not in their owners' *(masters)* hands
   gory: bloody
56 *discoloured:* unnaturally coloured (with blood)
58 *steeped:* covered
   unkind: unnatural
61 *comfortable:* providing spiritual comfort

Dies.

Enter FRIAR LAURENCE, *with a lantern, crow, and spade.*

FRIAR LAURENCE: Saint Francis be my speed! How oft tonight
35   Have my old feet stumbled at graves! Who's there?
BALTHASAR: Here's one, a friend, and one that knows you well.
FRIAR LAURENCE: Bliss be upon you! Tell me, good my friend,
    What torch is yond, that vainly lends his light
    To grubs and eyeless skulls? As I discern,
40   It burneth in the Capel's monument.
BALTHASAR: It doth so, holy sir; and there's my master,
    One that you love.
FRIAR LAURENCE: Who is it?
BALTHASAR: Romeo.
FRIAR LAURENCE: How long hath he been there?
BALTHASAR: Full half an hour.
FRIAR LAURENCE: Go with me to the vault.
BALTHASAR: I dare not, sir.
45   My master knows not but I am gone hence;
    And fearfully did menace me with death
    If I did stay to look on his intents.
FRIAR LAURENCE: Stay, then. I'll go alone. Fear comes upon me.
    O, much I fear some ill unlucky thing.
50 **BALTHASAR:** As I did sleep under this yew-tree here,
    I dreamt my master and another fought,
    And that my master slew him.
FRIAR LAURENCE: Romeo!

Advances.

    Alack, alack, what blood is this, which stains
    The stony entrance of this sepulchre?
55   What mean these masterless and gory swords
    To lie discoloured by this place of peace?

Enters the tomb.

    Romeo! O, pale! Who else? What, Paris too?
    And steeped in blood? Ah, what an unkind hour
    Is guilty of this lamentable chance!
60   The lady stirs.

JULIET *wakes.*

JULIET: O comfortable friar! Where is my lord?
    I do remember well where I should be,
    And there I am. Where is my Romeo?

Noise within.

65 *contagion:* ansteckende Krankheiten

  unnatural sleep: death

66 *contradict:* argue with

67 *thwarted:* destroyed, gone against

69 *dispose:* put away

75 *timeless:* occurring too early

76 *churl:* fool

77 *help me after:* help me follow you

78 *haply:* perhaps

79 *restorative:* a kiss that should have restored her to life

82 *happy:* well placed

83 *sheath:* Scheide

  rust: roste

86 *attach:* arrest

91 *raise up:* wake up

93 *true ground:* real reason

94 *circumstance:* all the facts surrounding the events

  descry [dɪˈskraɪ]: announce, make known

FRIAR LAURENCE: I hear some noise. Lady, come from that nest
65   Of death, contagion, and unnatural sleep.
    A greater power than we can contradict
    Hath thwarted our intents. Come, come away.
    Thy husband in thy bosom there lies dead;
    And Paris too. Come, I'll dispose of thee
70   Among a sisterhood of holy nuns.
    Stay not to question, for the watch is coming;
    Come, go, good Juliet, I dare no longer stay.

Exit FRIAR LAURENCE.

JULIET: Go, get thee hence, for I will not away.
    What's here? A cup, closed in my true love's hand?
75   Poison, I see, hath been his timeless end.
    O churl! Drunk all, and left no friendly drop
    To help me after? I will kiss thy lips.
    Haply some poison yet doth hang on them,
    To make die with a restorative.

Kisses him.

80   Thy lips are warm.
    1ST WATCHMAN: *[Within]* Lead, boy. Which way?
    JULIET: Yea, noise? Then I'll be brief. O happy dagger!

Taking ROMEO'S *dagger.*

    This is thy sheath;

Stabs herself.

                       there rust, and let me die.

Falls on ROMEO'S *body, and dies.*

Enter Watch, with the PAGE *of Paris.*

PAGE: This is the place. There, where the torch doth burn.
85   **1ST WATCHMAN:** The ground is bloody. Search about the churchyard.
    Go, some of you, whoe'er you find attach.
    Pitiful sight! Here lies the county slain,
    And Juliet bleeding, warm, and newly dead,
    Who here hath lain these two days burièd.
90   Go, tell the prince. Run to the Capulets.
    Raise up the Montagues. Some others search.
    We see the ground whereon these woes do lie;
    But the true ground of all these piteous woes
    We cannot without circumstance descry.

Re-enter some of the Watch, with BALTHASAR.

95   **2ND WATCHMAN:** Here's Romeo's man. We found him in the churchyard.

98 *mattock:* Spitzhacke

100 *a great suspicion:* very suspicious

     stay: hold

102 why are people making such a commotion so early

106 *with open outcry:* making a lot of noise, shouting a lot

108 *sovereign* ['sɒvrɪn]: ruler

110 *new:* recently

111 *comes:* happened, came about

116 *hath mista'en:* has mistaken its direction

     house: the cover of the dagger (which is on Romeo's side or back)

120 *warns:* summons

122 *early down:* prematurely dead

123 *liege* [liːdʒ]: lord

Note, l. 123: It is generally believed that Shakespeare added the death of the Lady Montague to allow the actor who played her very small part to be on stage in this scene in another role (e.g. Balthasar or Paris's page).

125 *conspires:* verschwört sich

127 *o thou untaught:* my ill-mannered son

128 *press:* rush

129 stop your expressions of passionate grief for a while

130 *ambiguities:* uncertainties

131 *spring:* Quelle

     their true descent: where they really come from

132 *general of your woes:* leader in expressing sadness

133 *even to death:* even if I die of sadness

     forbear: have patience

134 and let patience rule over misfortune

1ST WATCHMAN: Hold him in safety, till the prince come hither.

Re-enter others of the Watch, with FRIAR LAURENCE.

3RD WATCHMAN: Here is a friar, that trembles, sighs and weeps.
　　We took this mattock and this spade from him,
　　As he was coming from this churchyard side.
100　**1ST WATCHMAN:** A great suspicion. Stay the friar too.

Enter the PRINCE *and Attendants.*

PRINCE: What misadventure is so early up
　　That calls our person from our morning's rest?

Enter CAPULET, LADY CAPULET, *and others.*

CAPULET: What should it be that it is so shrieked abroad?
LADY CAPULET: The people in the street cry 'Romeo',
105　Some 'Juliet', and some 'Paris'; and all run,
　　With open outcry toward our monument.
PRINCE: What fear is this which startles in your ears?
1ST WATCHMAN: Sovereign, here lies the County Paris slain;
　　And Romeo dead; and Juliet, dead before,
110　Warm and new killed.
PRINCE: Search, seek, and know how this foul murder comes.
1ST WATCHMAN: Here is a friar, and slaughtered Romeo's man;
　　With instruments upon them, fit to open
　　These dead men's tombs.
115　**CAPULET:** O heavens! O wife, look how our daughter bleeds!
　　This dagger hath mista'en, for, lo, his house
　　Is empty on the back of Montague,
　　And it mis-sheathèd in my daughter's bosom!
LADY CAPULET: O me! This sight of death is as a bell,
120　That warns my old age to a sepulchre.

Enter MONTAGUE *and others.*

PRINCE: Come, Montague; for thou art early up,
　　To see thy son and heir more early down.
MONTAGUE: Alas, my liege, my wife is dead tonight.
　　Grief of my son's exìle hath stopped her breath.
125　What further woe conspires against mine age?
PRINCE: Look, and thou shalt see.
MONTAGUE: O thou untaught! What manners is in this
　　To press before thy father to a grave?
PRINCE: Seal up the mouth of outrage for a while,
130　Till we can clear these ambiguities,
　　And know their spring, their head, their true descent;
　　And then will I be general of your woes,
　　And lead you even to death. Meantime forbear,
　　And let mischance be slave to patience.

135 *parties of suspicion:* Verdächtige

136 *the greatest:* person most under suspicion

able to do least: the weakest and less likely (as he is old and a friar)

138 *doth make against me:* argues against me, implicates me

direful: terrible

139 *impeach:* accuse

purge: clear from guilt

142 *scourge:* Geißel, Plage

144 *winking at:* closing my eyes to

145 *brace:* number

147 *jointure:* marriage settlement following the death of one partner

– Capulet is saying that the hand of Montague he is holding (i.e. the sign of reconciliation) is all that he, as the father of the bride, can expect from the father of the bridegroom.

151 *figure:* statue

rate: value

153 *Romeo's:* Romeo's statue

155 *glooming:* gloomy

135 Bring forth the parties of suspicion.

FRIAR LAURENCE: I am the greatest, able to do least,
 Yet most suspected, as the time and place
 Doth make against me of this direful murder;
 And here I stand, both to impeach and purge
140 Myself condemnèd and myself excused.

The Friar relates everything that has happened, explaining that the secrecy was due to the feuding families.

PRINCE: Where be these enemies? Capulet! Montague!
 See, what a scourge is laid upon your hate,
 That heaven finds means to kill your joys with love.
 And I for winking at your discords too
145 Have lost a brace of kinsmen. All are punished.

CAPULET: O brother Montague, give me thy hand.
 This is my daughter's jointure, for no more
 Can I demand.

MONTAGUE: But I can give thee more:
 For I will raise her statue in pure gold;
150 That while Verona by that name is known,
 There shall no figure at such rate be set
 As that of true and faithful Juliet.

CAPULET: As rich shall Romeo's by his lady's lie.
 Poor sacrifices of our enmity!

155 **PRINCE:** A glooming peace this morning with it brings.
 The sun, for sorrow, will not show his head.
 Go hence, to have more talk of these sad things;
 Some shall be pardoned, and some punishèd;
 For never was a story of more woe
160 Than this of Juliet and her Romeo.

1 Point out Romeo's various thoughts in his final monologue (ll. 1–33).

2 Analyse the way Romeo talks about death by identifying and interpreting the metaphors.

3 Comment on the Friar's argumentation when he unsuccessfully tries to take Juliet out of the tomb (ll. 64–72).

4 Describe how the two strands of the plot, i.e. the star-crossed love and the ancient feud, are resolved through the final action.

5 Discuss the dramatic impact of the ending for the mood of the audience. Base your ideas on a close reading of the Prince's last words (ll. 155–160).

GENERAL QUESTIONS ON THE PLAY

1 Summarize the play in three sentences. Compare your summaries in small groups and decide on a version to present to the whole class.

2 Look back at the whole play and, in groups of four, analyse the structure with reference to the 'Infobox: Dramatic Structure' on p. 52, stating what events constitute
   – the rising action,
   – the climax,
   – the falling action
   – the catastrophe

3 The story of *Romeo and Juliet* is determined by the two elementary emotions of love and hate. Make two lists of events in the play that belong to one or the other emotion.
   Then put as many of them as possible in a mindmap or cluster to show how the items you have listed are actually connected in the play. You might want to write down the connection along the lines/ arrows connecting the items.

4 Evaluate how knowing and not knowing things influence the characters' behaviour throughout the play and lead to the succession of tragic events.

5 In l. 66 of the final scene Friar Laurence speaks of 'a greater power than we can contradict'; in the same scene (l. 24) just before his death, Romeo says he wants to 'shake the yoke of inauspicious stars'. Explain the image of the stars, and find further quotes from the play that underline the central role of fate for the play.

6 **a)** Write a character description of Juliet.

   b) With your description in mind, point out what it must have been like for a young man to play the part of a young woman like Juliet (cf. 'Infobox: Theatre in Shakespeare's Time', p. 14).

7 Evaluate the role of one of the following minor characters in the play:
   – Nurse
   – Friar Laurence
   – Mercutio

8 In a modern staging of *Romeo and Juliet* during the annual Shakespeare Festival at the Globe Theatre in Neuss, Germany, the actors drew lots (Lose) before each performance to determine which part they would play. Imagine you were one of these actors. Tell the class which part you would wish for, and which one you would hope not to draw, giving reasons to do with the characters and their behaviour.

9 *Romeo and Juliet* is often classified as the greatest love story of all time. Organize a debate in class with one side arguing for, the other strictly against this classification.

10 *Romeo and Juliet* has triggered a large amount of stories set in different places and different times. Do one of the following:

   a) Research on the Internet what 'modern versions' of the original Romeo-and-Juliet story exist, and what different backgrounds they deal with.

   b) Imagine a modern setting in which a story of 'star-crossed lovers' could take place, and in pairs write a story-line.